Our Earth

Use the diagram to complete the activity. For help, refer to page H11 in your textbook.

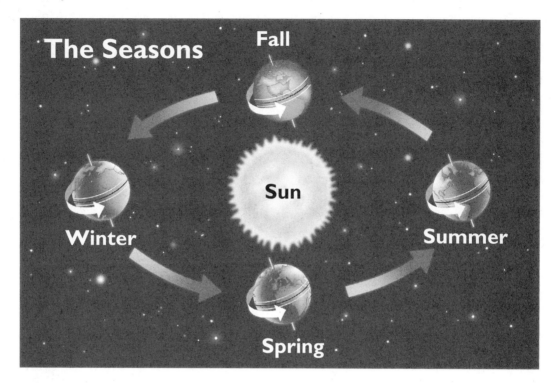

1. What does it mean to say that Earth revolves around the sun once each year?

   _____

   _____

2. Trace the arrows that show the path Earth takes as it revolves around the sun. Use a yellow crayon or marker.

3. Trace the arrows that show Earth rotating, or turning around on an axis. Use an orange crayon or marker.

4. What is an axis?

   _____

   _____

5. I am the longest day of the year in the Northern Hemisphere. Which day of the year am I?

   _____

6. Day and night are equal in length during my time, around March 21 and September 23. What am I?

   _____

7. What are solstices?

   _____

   _____

   _____

Understanding the Global Grid

Use the globe to complete the activity. For help, refer to page H12 in your textbook.

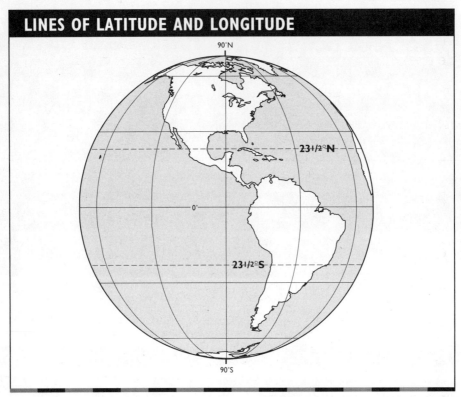

LINES OF LATITUDE AND LONGITUDE

90°N

23 1/2°N

0°

23 1/2°S

90°S

1. Label the following features on the globe:

   Equator   Tropic of Cancer
   North Pole   Tropic of Capricorn
   South Pole   60°E, 60°W
   South America   30°E, 30°W
   North America

2. Latitude lines run _____

   _____ .

3. Longitude lines run _____

   _____ .

4. Where do the lines of longitude meet?

   _____

   _____

5. Which continent does the equator cross?

   _____

   _____

6. Which continent lies north of the equator?

   _____

   _____

Use a Map

Use the map and map key to complete the activity. For help, refer to pages H13 to H15 in your textbook.

1. Jason lives in California. In which part of the United States is California? (Circle one)

   north   south   east   west

   What helped you find the answer?

   _____

   _____

2. Circle the capital of California.

   How did you identify the capital?

   _____

   _____

   _____

3. When Jason visits Mexico, he crosses this boundary. (Circle one)

   ━━━━━   ────

   What does this symbol represent?

   _____

4. Jason often visits California's national parks. His favorite is Yosemite National Park. In which direction is Yosemite National Park from Sacramento?

   _____

5. Which national parks are south of Yosemite?

   _____

   _____

6. What helped you locate those parks?

   _____

   _____

Explore a Map Scale

Use the map and map scale to complete the activity. For help,
refer to page H14 in your textbook.

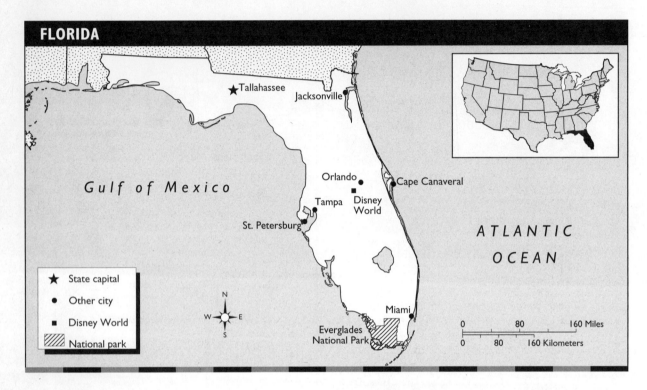

1. Mia visited Florida. In which part of the
   United States is Florida?

   _____

2. Mia rented a car and drove from
   Tampa to Disney World, near Orlando.
   In which direction did she travel?

   _____

   About how many miles did she travel?

   _____

3. After visiting Disney World, Mia drove
   to Cape Canaveral. In which direction
   did she travel?

   _____

4. About how many kilometers is
   Cape Canaveral from Orlando?

   _____

5. From Cape Canaveral, Mia drove to
   Miami. About how many miles is
   Miami from Cape Canaveral?

   _____

6. Mia took a train from Miami to
   Everglades National Park. In which
   direction is the park from Miami?

   _____

7. Mia flew from Miami to
   St. Petersburg. In which direction
   is St. Petersburg from Miami?

   _____

Discover a Political Map

Use the map to complete the activity. For help, refer to page H16 in your textbook.

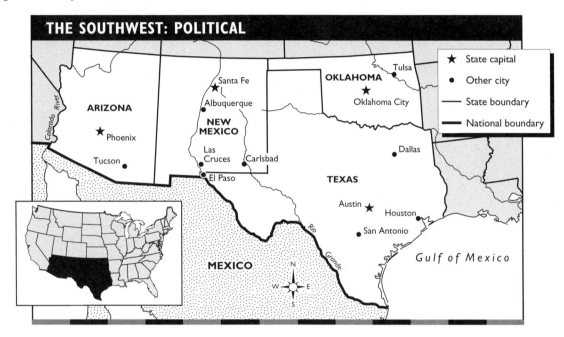

THE SOUTHWEST: POLITICAL

★ State capital
• Other city
— State boundary
━ National boundary

Tulsa

OKLAHOMA
★ Oklahoma City

Santa Fe ★
Albuquerque •

ARIZONA

NEW MEXICO

★ Phoenix

Las Cruces
Carlsbad

Tucson •

El Paso •

Dallas •

TEXAS

Austin ★
Houston •
San Antonio •

Colorado River

Rio Grande

MEXICO

N
W ● E
S

Gulf of Mexico

1. a. What kind of map is shown above?

_____

b. How do you know?

_____

_____

_____

2. Which states are shown in the subject area of the map?

_____

_____

3. Name the states and the countries located on the national boundary line.

_____

_____

_____

4. Which city is located on the border of the United States and Mexico?

_____

5. List the capital cities for the states shown on the map.

_____

_____

_____

_____

6. Which river runs along the national boundary line between the United States and Mexico?

_____

_____

Read a Physical and Climate Map

Use the maps to complete each activity.
For help, refer to pages 4 to 9 in your textbook.

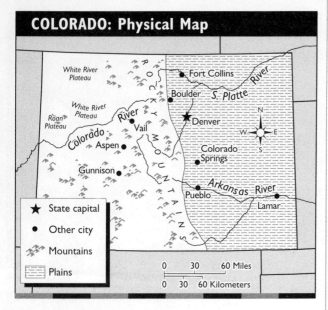

COLORADO: Physical Map

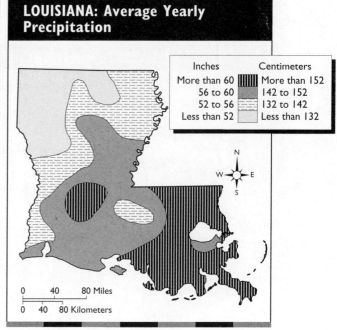

LOUISIANA: Average Yearly Precipitation

Inches		Centimeters
More than 60		More than 152
56 to 60		142 to 152
52 to 56		132 to 142
Less than 52		Less than 132

1. Why might you use this map? Check one answer.

   _____ to plan a car trip

   _____ to locate the Rocky Mountains

2. Name two kinds of landforms found in Colorado.

   _____

   _____

3. As you travel across Colorado from east to west, does the land become more or less mountainous?

   _____

4. If you were to travel from Lamar to Pueblo, would you drive through the mountains? Explain.

   _____

   _____

1. Is Louisiana in the arid or humid region of America? Explain.

   _____

   _____

   _____

   _____

   _____

   _____

2. Which part of Louisiana receives the least precipitation?

   _____

   _____

3. Which part of Louisiana receives the most precipitation?

   _____

   _____

Name: _____   Date: _____

Exploring Latitude and Longitude

Use the map to complete the activity. For help, refer to
pages 10 and 11 in your textbook.

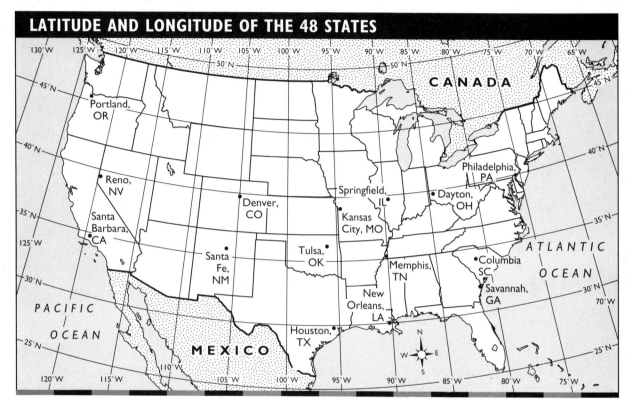

LATITUDE AND LONGITUDE OF THE 48 STATES

1. The Greene family traveled across the United States. They stopped at eight
   cities. The list below gives the lines of latitude and longitude closest to each
   city. Find each city on the map. Then draw a line following the route that the
   Greene family took.

first city:	45°N, 125°W	**fifth city:**	30°N, 90°W
second city:	35°N, 120°W	**sixth city:**	30°N, 80°W
third city:	35°N, 105°W	**seventh city:**	35°N, 80°W
fourth city:	30°N, 95°W	**eighth city:**	40°N, 75°W

2. On their way home the Greenes stopped at the cities listed below. Find and
   circle each city on the map. Then write the lines of latitude and longitude
   closest to each city.

City	**Latitude and Longitude**
Springfield, Illinois	_____
Denver, Colorado	_____
Reno, Nevada	_____

Our Natural Resources

Use the picture below to complete the activity. For help, refer to pages 12 to 15 in your textbook.

1. Paper is made from trees. Which natural resource did the boys use in making their airplanes?

   _____

2. Name two other objects in the picture that are made from this natural resource.

   _____

3. Which word describes a major threat to this natural resource? (Circle one)

   ecosystems   pollution   soil

4. List three ways this natural resource benefits people.

   _____

   _____

   _____

5. Name four other kinds of natural resources found in the United States.

   _____

6. What is conservation? _____

   _____

Problem Solving

Read and complete the activity below.
For help, refer to pages 16 and 17 in your textbook.

1. Put the 6 steps in problem solving in order, from
   Step 1 through Step 6.

   Step _____ Identify the options.

   Step _____ Gather information.

   Step _____ Choose a solution.

   Step _____ Identify the problem.

   Step _____ List the possible consequences.

   Step _____ Evaluate the solution.

2. Liz would like to do something to help the environment, but she doesn't know what to do.
   She decides to visit the library. During her visit Liz wrote the following in her notebook:

   Less Junk Mail, Please!
   Junk mail hurts the environment. One family can get as many as 30 pieces of junk
   mail each week. That is a mountain of paper. After people throw it away, the
   junk mail goes to landfills. It takes years for it to decompose.

   Which step in problem solving is Liz probably working on? Explain your answer.

   _____

   _____

   _____

3. Liz has identified some options, or ways, to help limit junk mail.

   • Write to companies that send out junk mail. Explain the problem. Ask
     them to stop sending out so much junk mail.

   • Create a web site giving people tips on how to reuse and recycle junk
     mail.

   • Make a video. Explain how people can stop junk mail from coming to their
     homes. Set up the video in main lobby of the school. Play it continuously
     for all to see.

   What is the next step in problem solving facing Liz?

   _____

   _____

Name: _____ Date: _____

Looking at Immigration

Use the graphs to complete the activity. For help, refer to pages 18 to 21 in your textbook.

Immigration to the United States

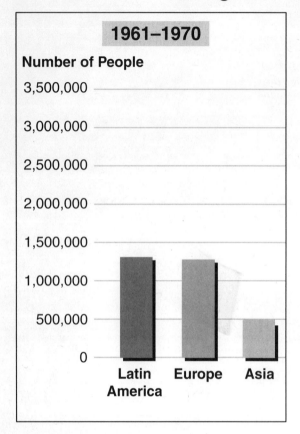

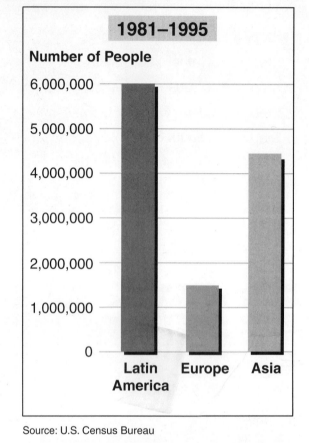

Source: U.S. Census Bureau

1. Which parts of the world are represented in the graphs?

   _____

   _____

   _____

2. From where did the fewest immigrants come between 1961 and 1970?

   _____

3. From where did the fewest immigrants come between 1981 and 1995?

   _____

4. From which part of the world did the most immigrants come between the years 1981 to 1995?

   _____

5. What do the graphs tell you about population growth in the United States?

   _____

   _____

   _____

   _____

©Macmillan/McGraw-Hill

Understanding Our Government

Read the paragraph below. Then answer the questions. For help, refer to pages 22 and 23 in your textbook.

Preamble to the Constitution of the United States

We the People of the United States, in order to form a more perfect Union, establish justice, insure domestic tranquility, provide for the common defense, promote the general welfare, and secure the blessings of liberty to ourselves and our posterity, do ordain and establish this Constitution for the United States of America.

1. Was the Preamble written to begin or end the Constitution?

    _____

2. What plan does the Constitution lay out?

    _____

    _____

3. Which kind of government did the Constitution establish for our country?

    _____

4. Which phrase in the Preamble shows that the founders of our country believed in democracy?

    _____

    _____

5. What role do people play in a democracy?

    _____

    _____

6. How do American citizens choose representatives to run the government?

    _____

    _____

7. For which three levels of government do American citizens choose representatives?

    _____

    _____

    _____

8. The Constitution protects the individual rights of people living in the United States. What are these rights called?

    _____

    Give two examples of these rights.

    _____

    _____

Writing an Outline

Write an outline for a report on the environment using the notes below.
For help, refer to pages 24 and 25 in your textbook.

NOTES

• Mining, logging, and industry

• Six major kinds of ecosystems

• Ways to conserve our natural resources

• Renewable natural resources

• Things that harm ecosystems

• The growth of urban and suburban areas

• Nonrenewable natural resources

• Laws to protect the environment

OUTLINE

I. Ecosystems

   A. _____

   B. _____

II. Natural Resources

   A. _____

   B. _____

III. Changing the Land

   A. _____

   B. _____

IV. Conservation

   A. _____

   B. _____

In Economic Terms

Read the following and answer the questions. Explain your answers.
For help, refer to pages 26 and 27 in your textbook.

1. José reads an ad in the local newspaper announcing Customer-Appreciation Week at the mall. The ad lists some of the things on sale during that week. José finds his favorite jeans on the list. He hopes to have enough money saved to buy a pair.

   Which economic term best describes José? (Circle one) Explain.

   consumer   producer   entrepreneur

   _____

   _____

   _____

2. Hannah's friends often complain about not having anything to do on the weekend. She decides to put out an entertainment newsletter each week. In it she'll list movies, museum exhibits, sports events, and plays for kids. She'll charge one dollar for a five-week subscription.

   Which economic term best describes Hannah? (Circle one) Explain.

   free enterprise   entrepreneur   consumer

   _____

   _____

   _____

3. What is a free enterprise system?

   _____

   _____

   _____

Identifying Historical Sources

Read the paragraph on the right. Then answer the questions on the left.
For help, refer to pages 28 and 29 in your textbook.

1. a. This paragraph is from a textbook written in 1986. The authors describe how immigrants to the United States in the late 1800s gathered in ethnic neighborhoods in big cities. Is it a primary source or a secondary source?

_____

b. How do you know?

_____

_____

_____

In cities such as Chicago they *[immigrants]* formed ethnic and national neighborhoods. When the Poles settled in Chicago, an area called "Little Poland" appeared. When Chinese people settled in San Francisco, "Chinatown" appeared. In New York City, Italians created "Little Italy" on Mulberry Street. Jewish families from Eastern Europe gathered together in New York's Lower East Side.

John Patrick and Carol Berkin, *History of the American Nation from 1877,* Vol. 2 (New York: Macmillan, 1986), page 511.

2. a. This paragraph is a quote from Yusef Arbeely as he talked to a reporter in 1881 about being in America. Yusef Arbeely and his family had immigrated to the United States from Damascus, Syria. Is it a primary source or a secondary source?

_____

b. How do you know?

_____

_____

_____

The change from Damascus, almost the oldest city in the world, to this, the newest and most active civilization in the world, was very great. But I have not been disappointed. I left my relatives and friends behind because I desired freedom of speech and action and educational advantages for my children. In coming here I have escaped the disadvantages of a . . . tyrannical government, and have found all that I came in search of.

John Patrick and Carol Berkin, *History of the American Nation from 1877,* Vol. 2 (New York: Macmillan, 1986), page 30.

3. Why is it important to look at the history of our country's people?

_____

_____

©Macmillan/McGraw-Hill

Identifying Our Nation's Regions

Use the map to complete the activity. For help, refer to pages 30 and 31 in your textbook.

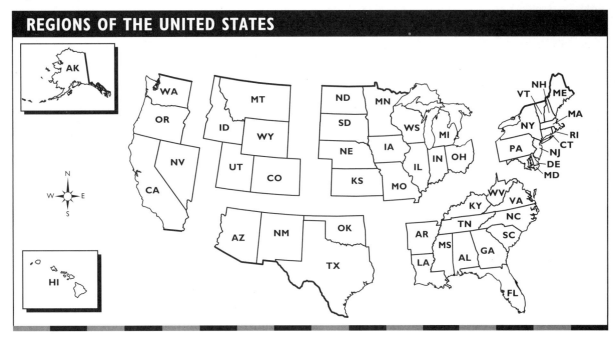

REGIONS OF THE UNITED STATES

1. Use the following words to label each region on the map.

   Southwest   Middle West

   Southeast   Northeast

   West   Mountain States

2. Each region is a mixture of physical and cultural features. (Circle one)

   True   False

3. Which region has redwood forests?

   _____

4. Which southeastern state is farthest north?

   _____

5. Which two regions have the same number of states?

   _____

6. To which region do Alaska and Hawaii belong?

   _____

7. Which region is home to the Gullah people?

   _____

8. Name two economic regions in the United States.

   _____

   _____

Matching Words and Their Meanings

Match each term in the box with its meaning. For help, refer to the lessons in the Introduction of your textbook.

a. ecosystem	**h.** ethnic group	**o.** democratic republic
b. federal government	**i.** consumer	**p.** environment
c. free enterprise	**j.** historian	**q.** values
d. entrepreneurs	**k.** constitution	**r.** renewable resources
e. citizen	**l.** immigrant	**s.** nonrenewable resources
f. conservation	**m.** diversity	**t.** climate
g. cultural regions	**n.** secondary source	

_____ 1. a system allowing people to own land and operate businesses

_____ 2. resources that cannot be replaced

_____ 3. the surroundings in which people, plants, and animals live

_____ 4. the weather an area has throughout the year

_____ 5. an account of the past written by someone who was not an eyewitness to those events

_____ 6. a group of people who share the same customs and language

_____ 7. a person who is born in a country or who becomes a member of a country by law

_____ 8. national government

_____ 9. areas where people share the same customs, beliefs, and language

_____ 10. the protection and careful use of natural resources

_____ 11. the beliefs and ideals that guide the way people live

_____ 12. variety

_____ 13. a system in which people choose representatives to run the government

_____ 14. a person who buys and uses goods and services

_____ 15. resources that can be replaced

_____ 16. a plan of government

_____ 17. all the living and nonliving things in a certain area

_____ 18. a person who studies the past

_____ 19. people who use their ideas to start a business

_____ 20. a person who comes to a country from another to live

©Macmillan/McGraw-Hill

Looking at the Maya

Answer the questions to complete the activity. For help, refer to pages 40 to 45 in your textbook.

1. The picture above shows an ancient Maya structure hundreds of feet tall. What is the structure? Why did the Maya build such structures?

_____

_____

2. In which present-day countries did the ancient Maya live?

_____

3. What kind of data did the Maya write down?

_____

_____

4. What talents did the Maya have?

_____

_____

5. What is a civilization?

_____

_____

Read a Time Line

Read the time line and the questions below it. Put an **X** next to each true statement. For help, refer to pages 46 and 47 in your textbook.

Maya Culture

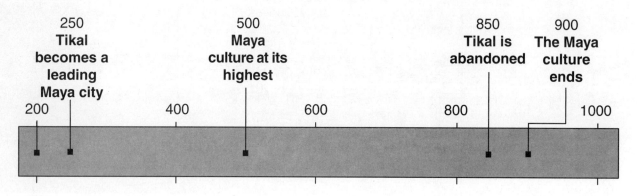

_____ 1. The time line covers a period of 800 years.

_____ 2. In 250 Tikal became a leading Maya city.

_____ 3. Tikal was an important Maya city for about 600 years.

_____ 4. The Maya culture ended about 750 years after it began.

_____ 5. The Maya culture reached its highest point in the third century.

_____ 6. Tikal was abandoned around 850.

_____ 7. Maya culture was at its high point in 500.

What is a time line?

_____

_____

How can a time line help you?

_____

_____

Exploring Tenochtitlán

Complete the activity by answering five questions. For help, refer to pages 48 to 51 in your textbook.

The Island City of Tenochtitlán

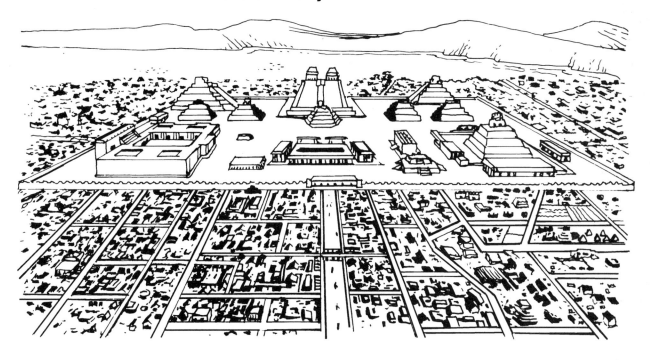

1. What empire had Tenochtitlán as its capital?

_____

_____

2. On what kind of land was Tenochtitlán built?

_____

_____

3. In which present-day country was Tenochtitlán built?

_____

_____

4. The Aztec built many bridges and causeways. Why was this so?

_____

_____

5. Explain how the Aztec culture was both beautiful and cruel.

_____

_____

_____

_____

Using New Words

Use a word from the box to complete each sentence. For help, refer to the lessons in Chapter 1 of your textbook.

Ice Ages	slavery	irrigation	empire
civilization	glaciers	specialize	

1. If you described a large area of different groups of people controlled by one ruler or government, you would be describing an _____.

2. If you described a method by which water is brought into dry areas, you would be describing a system of _____.

3. If you referred to people who spend most of their time doing one kind of job, you would be referring to people who _____.

4. To describe a culture that has developed complex systems of government, education, and religion, you might use the word _____.

5. In describing the time when Earth went through periods of extreme cold, you might use the term _____.

6. In discussing a time when most of Earth's water was frozen into huge sheets of ice, you would call these sheets of ice _____.

7. If you described the practice of forcing people to work without pay and without freedom, you would be describing _____.

©Macmillan/McGraw-Hill

Observing Hopi Life

Use the pictures on the right to complete the activity. For help, refer to pages 56 to 61 in your textbook.

1. a. Draw a line to the picture that shows how the Hopi used adobe.

    b. What makes adobe a good building material?

_____

_____

_____

2. a. Draw a line to the picture that shows the Hopi growing crops.

    b. Describe the Hopi method of farming.

_____

_____

_____

3. a. Draw a line to the picture that shows a Hopi religious ceremony.

    b. Who are the kachinas and why are they important?

_____

_____

_____

_____

Kachina Ceremony

Dry Farming

Pueblo

The Iroquois Confederacy

Use the map and pages 62 to 67 in your textbook to complete the activity. Mark each statement true or false. Then explain your answer.

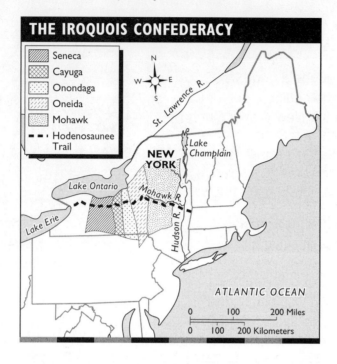

1. The Eastern Woodlands provide the Iroquois with abundant natural resources.

_____

_____

2. The Hodenosaunee Trail connected the five major Iroquois peoples.

_____

_____

3. Women had very little power in the Iroquois world. _____

_____

_____

_____

4. The Iroquois formed the Iroquois Confederacy to become more powerful. _____

_____

_____

Our Nation

Practice and Activity

Identifying Cause and Effect

The paragraph tells the story of how the horse changed life for Native Americans of the plains. Read the story. Then circle the answer. For help, refer to pages 68 and 69 in your textbook.

Horses were unknown in North America until the 1500s, when Spanish explorers began arriving. The explorers sailed from Spain with horses onboard their ships. They used the horses to explore the New World. During this exploration many of the Spanish horses were lost. They were left to roam free and become wild. Later, plains people, such as the Lakota, began catching and taming the wild horses. These people became expert riders, trainers, and breeders. They found that traveling on horseback was much faster and easier than on foot. As a result, they began hunting buffalo year-round. Soon buffalo meat replaced crops as the main source of food. Buffalo hide became an important source of clothing and building materials. Eventually, plains people abandoned their permanent settlements. They began moving from one campsite to another following the buffalo herds.

1. What is the main cause-and-effect relationship expressed in the paragraph?

    a. horses changed life for the Plains peoples

    b. the Spanish brought horses to North America

    c. horses became wild when left to roam free

2. Why were Native Americans able to begin following the buffalo herds?

    a. they gave up farming

    b. wild horses roamed the plains

    c. horses made travel faster and easier

3. What word clue in the paragraph helped you figure out the answer to question 2?

    a. because

    b. since

    c. as a result

4. Why is it important to understand cause-and-effect connections?

    _____

    _____

    _____

    _____

    _____

©Macmillan/McGraw-Hill

Talking with a Lakota Chief

Try to imagine what it was like to be Chief Standing Bear, of the Oglala Lakota. How would you answer the questions below? Write your answers in the space provided. For help, refer to pages 70 to 75 in your textbook.

Question: In which part of the Great Plains do you live?

Standing Bear: _____

_____

Question: Please describe the land and climate of the Great Plains.

Standing Bear: _____

_____

Question: Large herds of buffalo roam the Great Plains. What part does the buffalo play in the life of your people?

Standing Bear: _____

_____

Question: How do you keep track of important events?

Standing Bear: _____

_____

_____

_____

Question: Will you describe how you train your children?

Standing Bear: _____

_____

_____

_____

Question: How did the horse change life for Native Americans living on the Great Plains?

Standing Bear: _____

_____

_____

©Macmillan/McGraw-Hill

Name: _____   Date: _____

Thinking About the Tlingit

Use the picture below to complete the activity. For help, refer to pages 76 to 81 in your textbook.

1. The picture shows how daily life among the Tlingit might have looked long ago. Where did this group of Native Americans live? Circle your answer.

   Northwest Coast   Southern California   Great Basin

2. Why was salmon an important resource for the Tlingit?

   _____

   _____

3. Circle two examples of Tlingit technology. What allowed the Tlingit to develop

   technology? _____

   _____

4. Draw a box around an example of Tlingit art. What is the art object called and why was

   it built? _____

   _____

5. How did the Tlingit preserve their culture after their homeland became part of the

   United States? _____

   _____

   _____

©Macmillan/McGraw-Hill

Matching Words and Their Meanings

Correct the terms with a definition. Write the letter in the space provided.
For help, refer to the lessons in Chapter 2 of your textbook.

a. adobe	**f.** longhouse	**k.** compromise	**p.** jerky
b. lodge	**g.** wampum	**l.** Iroquois Confederacy	**q.** kachinas
c. teepee	**h.** totem pole	**m.** clan	**r.** kiva
d. pueblo	**i.** coup stick	**n.** prairie	**s.** hogan
e. potlatch	**j.** technology	**o.** travois	

_____ 1. the design and use of tools, ideas, and methods to solve problems

_____ 2. a tall log carved with many designs

_____ 3. a special Tlingit feast at which guests, not hosts, receive gifts

_____ 4. a Spanish word that means "village"

_____ 5. a type of clay found in the earth

_____ 6. spirits that the Hopi believe bring rain, help crops grow, show people how to live and behave, and bring peace and prosperity

_____ 7. thin strips of dried meat

_____ 8. a flat or gently rolling land covered mostly with grasses and wildflowers

_____ 9. a cone-shaped tent made of animal skins

_____ 10. a sled-like device used for carrying people and belongings

_____ 11. a special weapon used by the Lakota to touch an enemy without killing him

_____ 12. a home made of logs covered with grasses, sticks, and soil

_____ 13. dome-shaped dwellings with log frames that are covered with mud or sod

_____ 14. a long building made of poles covered with sheets of bark

_____ 15. small, polished beads that were usually made of shells and strung or woven together

_____ 16. a group of families who share the same ancestor

_____ 17. the union of five separate Iroquois peoples for a common purpose

_____ 18. the settling of disputes by agreeing that each side will give up part of its demands

_____ 19. a round structure used for religious ceremonies

Marco Polo

Answer the questions to complete the activity. For help, refer to pages 96 to 101 in your textbook.

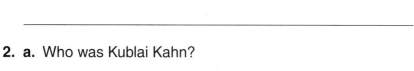

1. Marco Polo was one of the first Europeans to travel to China. Which route did he take?

_____

_____

Marco Polo

2. a. Who was Kublai Kahn?

_____

b. Describe Kublai Kahn's relationship with Marco Polo.

_____

_____

_____

3. a. How did Europeans of the time come to learn of Marco Polo's travels in the East?

_____

_____

_____

b. How do people today know about Marco Polo's adventures?

_____

_____

4. a. How did Marco Polo's travels influence Europe?

_____

_____

_____

b. Which historical period did Marco Polo's travels inspire?

_____

Reading Graphs

In the early 1400s China's rulers built a fleet of ships. They used the ships to explore areas beyond China's borders. The graphs below give information about this fleet. Use the graphs to complete the activity. Circle the answer to each question. For help, refer to pages 102 and 103 in your textbook.

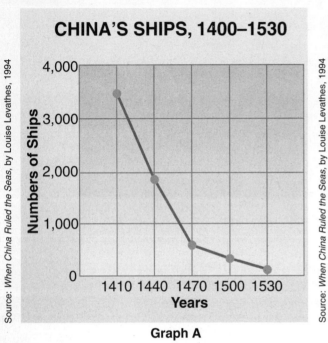

Source: *When China Ruled the Seas*, by Louise Levathes, 1994

Graph A

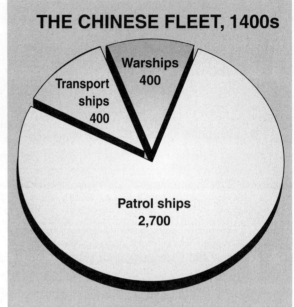

Source: *When China Ruled the Seas*, by Louise Levathes, 1994

Graph B

1. Which graph is a line graph?

   Graph A   Graph B

2. Which graph shows how many ships China had in 1500?

   Graph A   Graph B

3. Which graph tells about the different kinds of ships in the Chinese fleet?

   Graph A   Graph B

4. In which year did China have the most ships?

   1410   1440   1470

   1500   1530

5. Which graph did you use to answer question 4?

   Graph A   Graph B

6. How many transport ships did the Chinese have in the early 1400s?

   400   2,700

7. Which graph did you use to answer question 6?

   Graph A   Graph B

8. How many ships were in the Chinese fleet in 1410?

   2,700   1,900   3,500

©Macmillan/McGraw-Hill

Trade and the Songhai Empire

Use the map to complete the activity below. For help, refer to pages 104 to 107 in your textbook.

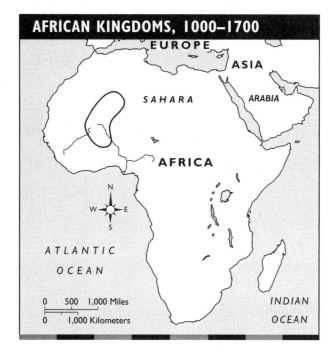

AFRICAN KINGDOMS, 1000–1700

1. **a.** Label the kingdom of Songhai. Color it in red.

   b. Who was king of Songhai in 1464?

   _____

   c. How did this king influence Songhai?

   _____

   _____

2. **a.** Make a dot to show the location of Timbuktu. Then label the city.

   b. Why was this city important to Songhai?

   _____

   _____

   _____

   _____

3. **a.** Draw a caravan route from Arabia to Timbuktu.

   b. List the parts of the world outside of Africa to which trade routes like this one led.

   _____

4. **a.** Which two trade goods helped make Songhai the most powerful kingdom in Africa?

   _____

   b. From which areas of Africa did these goods come?

   _____

   _____

©Macmillan/McGraw-Hill

Early European Explorers

Use the pictures on the right to help you complete the activity.
For help, refer to pages 108 to 111 in your textbook.

1. a. Draw a line to the first explorer to sail
around the southern tip of Africa.

   b. What did he call this area?

   _____

   _____

   c. What information did he bring back to
   Europe from Asia?

   _____

   _____

   _____

Prince Henry

2. a. Draw a line to the explorer who made it
possible to reach Asia by ship.

   b. How did he accomplish this?

   _____

   _____

   _____

Vasco da Gama

   c. Why did European traders want to find a
   sea route to Asia?

   _____

   _____

3. a. Draw a line to the first explorer to reach
Asia by ship.

   b. What did his voyage show European
   traders?

   _____

   _____

Bartolomeu Dias

Finding and Using New Words

Seven terms are hidden among the letters in the box. They may be read forward, backward, up, or down. Circle each word. Then write the word in the space before its definition. For help, refer to Chapter 3 of your textbook.

E	M	A	G	N	E	T	I	C	C	O	M	P	A	S	S	E
S	G	S	K	L	B	L	N	A	V	I	G	A	T	I	O	N
P	V	E	P	E	P	P	E	R	L	K	C	E	R	L	E	E
I	N	O	C	A	V	S	G	A	Y	I	O	N	A	K	G	W
C	B	D	T	E	R	C	U	V	H	L	E	V	A	R	A	C
E	B	A	L	O	R	T	S	A	K	L	S	E	V	O	L	C
S	C	N	E	Y	J	I	W	N	E	R	S	R	M	A	T	A
B	L	A	S	T	X	O	L	Y	B	E	P	U	J	D	W	F

_____ 1. two spices used during the Middle Ages to preserve food

_____ 2. an overland trade route to the East used during the Middle Ages

_____ 3. a small ship that was fast and easy to steer, even in dangerous waters

_____ 4. a group of people traveling together, especially through desert areas

_____ 5. an instrument that helps sailors and other travelers find the cardinal directions

_____ 6. the science of determining a ship's direction and location

Columbus's Expeditions

Use the map on this page to complete the activity below.
For help, refer to pages 116 to 125 in your textbook.

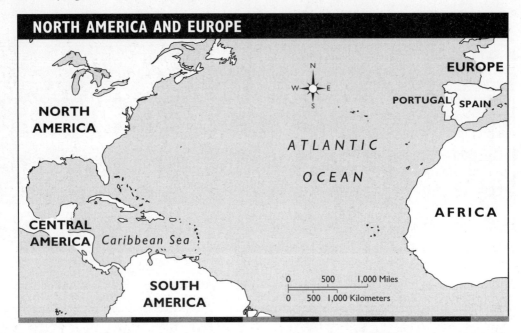

1. Draw the route Columbus took on his first expedition to the Americas.

2. Why did Columbus make this expedition?

   _____

   _____

   _____

3. Locate the group of islands Columbus reached during his first expedition. Label them.

4. What did Columbus name the first island he visited in the Americas?

   _____

5. Label this island on the map.

6. What do historians call the movement of people, plants, animals, and germs caused by Columbus's expeditions?

   _____

7. Describe a change in the Eastern Hemisphere caused by this movement.

   _____

   _____

   _____

   _____

   _____

8. List two changes in the Americas caused by this movement.

   _____

   _____

   _____

   _____

The Fall of an Aztec City

The excerpt was written by the European explorer Hernando Cortés during his conquest of the Aztec city of Tenochtitlán. Read the paragraph and complete the activity. For additional background, refer to pages 128 to 135 in your textbook.

It *[the religious center]* is so large that in its precincts, which are surrounded by a wall, there could well lie a settlement of five hundred. Inside this area, about its edges, are fine buildings with large halls and corridors. There are at least 40 pyramids, very tall and well made; the largest has 50 steps leading up to the main body of the pyramid. . . . The stone masonry and the woodwork are equally good; they could nowhere be bettered. All the stonework inside the temples where they keep the idols is sculptured, and the woodwork is all carved in relief and painted with pictures of monsters and other figures and designs.

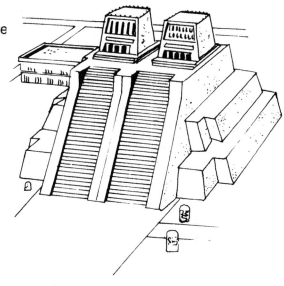

Editors, Time-Life Books, *Aztecs: Reign of Blood & Splendor* (Alexandria, VA: Time-Life Books, 1992).

1. How did Cortés feel about what he had seen at Tenochtitlán?

_____

_____

2. Who was the Aztec emperor during Cortés' conquest? _____

What happened to him? _____

_____

3. List two reasons Cortés was able to conquer the Aztec empire.

_____

4. What happened to Tenochtitlán after it fell to Cortés?

_____

_____

5. What did the Spanish call the new colony they set up on the site of Tenochtitlán?

_____

6. What modern city is located where Tenochtitlán once stood? _____

©Macmillan/McGraw-Hill

Reading Historical Maps

The map below shows the routes taken by the Spanish as they explored North America. Use the map to complete the activity. For help, refer to pages 136 and 137 in your textbook.

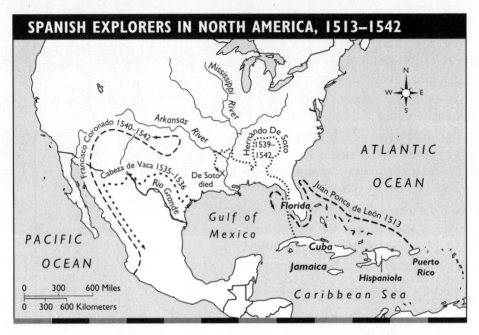

SPANISH EXPLORERS IN NORTH AMERICA, 1513–1542

1. List two features that tell you this is a historical map.

   _____

   _____

   _____

2. List the names of the explorers whose routes are shown on the map.

   _____

   _____

   _____

3. Which major river did Hernando De Soto cross?

   _____

4. Circle the part of North America Francisco Coronado explored.

   southeast   southwest

   northeast   northwest

5. During which years did Cabeza de Vaca explore Mexico?

   _____

6. Which present-day state did Ponce de León explore? In which year?

   _____

   From which island in the Caribbean Sea did Ponce de Leon sail to the North American continent?

   _____

©Macmillan/McGraw-Hill

Life in New Spain

Read each picture and caption. Then use the space provided to describe what life was like in New Spain for the people shown. For help, refer to pages 138 to 145 in your textbook.

_____

_____

_____

_____

_____

_____

_____

_____

_____

_____

_____

_____

_____

_____

_____

_____

_____

_____

_____

Indians of New Spain live and work on encomiendas.

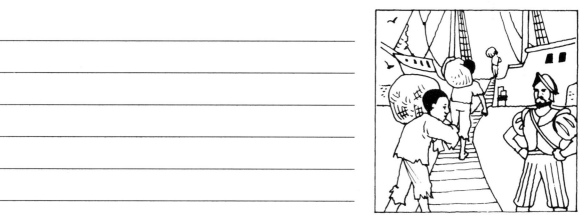

Enslaved Africans load a cargo ship.

A Spanish couple explore a plaza in Mexico City.

Our Nation

Practice and Activity

Finding and Using New Words

Find the term hidden in each group of letters. Write the term on the line.

1. Cross out these letters: d, e, f, g. _____

   e f c g d o l e f d o e n g y

2. Cross out these letters: g, l, p, s. _____

   s e n l c g o m p s l i e n g d s l a

3. Cross out these letters: a, b, c. _____

   a b l a c b o c c g a

4. Cross out these letters: d, e, g, u. _____

   d e m i g u s e d s i o d u g n d a r e u y

5. Cross out these letters: f, k, p. _____

   f C o k p l u p m b f i a k n E p x c h k a f n g p k e

6. Cross out these letters: b, e, w. _____

   c w e o n e b q e u i s e w t b a d e o w r

Write each word revealed above next to the appropriate meaning. For help, refer to Chapter 4 in your textbook.

_____   7. a record of a voyage

_____   8. a settlement far away from the country that rules it

_____   9. the movement of people, plants, animals, and germs across the Atlantic Ocean during the time of Columbus

_____   10. a soldier who conquered new lands for Spain

_____   11. a large piece of land granted by Spain to certain Spanish colonists

_____   12. a person who teaches his or her religion to others who have different beliefs

©Macmillan/McGraw-Hill

The Search for a Northwest Passage

Use the map to complete the activity below. For help, refer to pages 150 to 155 in your textbook.

1. In red draw the route Henry Hudson took in 1609 to explore the coast of North America.

2. Label the two bays that Hudson saw.

3. In blue trace the river Hudson sailed. What is this river called today?

   _____

4. What was Hudson searching for on his voyage?

   _____

   _____

5. Who paid for Hudson's expedition and why?

   _____

   _____

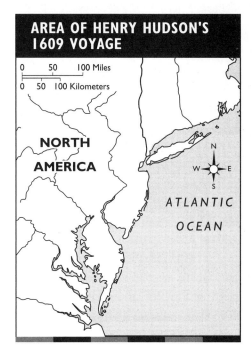

AREA OF HENRY HUDSON'S 1609 VOYAGE

0   50   100 Miles
0   50   100 Kilometers

NORTH AMERICA

ATLANTIC OCEAN

6. Describe how the Dutch financed Hudson's expedition.

   _____

   _____

   _____

7. What happened as a result of European exploration of the east coast of North America?

   _____

   _____

   _____

©Macmillan/McGraw-Hill

Making Decisions

In studying the history of local Native Americans, Rob's class will take a field trip. The class was offered three choices. Tomorrow students will vote on where to go. Read how Rob decided for which trip to vote. Then answer the questions. For help, refer to pages 156 and 157 in your textbook.

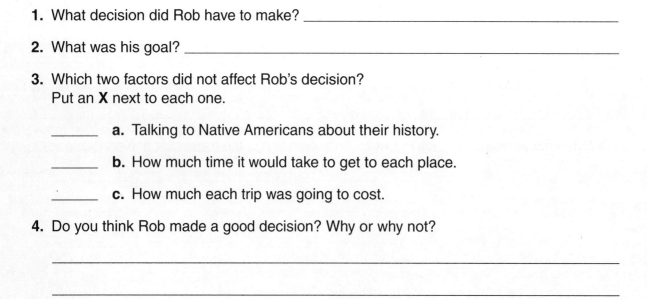

Our first choice is a local Native American village. There I could see how Native Americans live today. I could speak with the Native Americans about their history.

The second choice is the natural history museum. The museum has many Native American displays. But there wouldn't be any Native Americans with which to talk. Only a few displays are about local Native Americans.

The third choice is a Native American crafts fair. There will be many interesting things to see and buy. But I've already been to the fair once. Besides, there probably won't be any experts on Native American history.

The more I think about it, the better the Native American village sounds. I can see how the people live today. I can learn about history from the Native Americans themselves.

1. What decision did Rob have to make? _____

2. What was his goal? _____

3. Which two factors did not affect Rob's decision?
   Put an **X** next to each one.

   _____ **a.** Talking to Native Americans about their history.

   _____ **b.** How much time it would take to get to each place.

   _____ **c.** How much each trip was going to cost.

4. Do you think Rob made a good decision? Why or why not?

   _____

   _____

   _____

   _____

©Macmillan/McGraw-Hill

The Lost Colony

Use the information in the box to make a chart of important events about Roanoke Island. Then answer the questions that follow. For help, refer to pages 158 to 163 in your textbook.

> - Sir Walter Raleigh sends John White and a second group of colonists to Roanoke Island. That same year John White returns to England for supplies.
> - John White returns to Roanoke with supplies. He had been delayed by England's war with Spain. On his return, White discovers that the colonists have vanished.
> - Sir Walter Raleigh sends the first English colonists to Roanoke Island. The colonists soon return to England.

| IMPORTANT EVENTS IN THE SETTLEMENT OF ROANOKE ISLAND ||
DATE	EVENT
1585	
1587	
1590	

1. About how many years passed between the arrival of the two groups of colonists on

   Roanoke Island? _____

2. Why was John White's return to Roanoke Island delayed? _____

   _____

   About how many years was he delayed? _____

3. What do you think might have happened to the colonists? _____

   _____

   _____

Plymouth in the News

The headlines below might have appeared in English newspapers during the early 1600s. Read the headlines and answer the questions. For help, refer to pages 164 to 169 in your textbook.

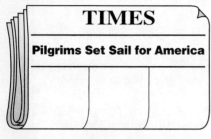
TIMES
Pilgrims Set Sail for America

TIMES
Pilgrims Sign Mayflower Compact

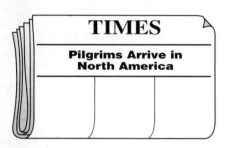
TIMES
Pilgrims Arrive in North America

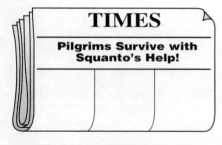
TIMES
Pilgrims Survive with Squanto's Help!

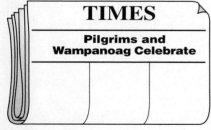
TIMES
Pilgrims and Wampanoag Celebrate

1. Why did the Pilgrims leave England?

_____

_____

2. What was the Mayflower Compact? Why was it important?

_____

_____

_____

3. Why did the Pilgrims settle in New England?

_____

_____

_____

4. Who was Squanto? How did he help the Pilgrims?

_____

_____

_____

5. Why did the Pilgrims and the Wampanoag celebrate? What do we call this celebration today?

_____

_____

_____

Using New Words

Use the code in the box to figure out the words. Then write the number of each word next to its meaning. For help, refer to Chapter 5 of your textbook.

a = 26	e = 24	i = 22	m = 20	q = 18	u = 16	y = 14
b = 1	f = 3	j = 5	n = 7	r = 9	v = 11	z = 13
c = 25	g = 23	k = 21	o = 19	s = 17	w = 15	
d = 2	h = 4	l = 6	p = 8	t = 10	x = 12	

1. 17 10 19 25 21

_____

2. 25 26 17 4   25 9 19 8

_____

3. 20 26 14 3 6 19 15 24 9
25 19 20 8 26 25 10

_____

4. 7 19 9 10 4 15 24 17 10
8 26 17 17 26 23 24

_____

5. 26 9 20 26 2 26

_____

6. 4 19 16 17 24   19 3
1 16 9 23 24 17 17 24 17

_____

7. 17 26 25 4 24 20

_____

8. 22 7 2 24 7 10 16 9 24 2
17 24 9 11 26 7 10

_____

9. 8 9 19 3 22 10

_____

_____ **a.** a large fleet of ships

_____ **b.** a water route through North America to Asia

_____ **c.** the amount of money remaining after the costs of a business have been paid

_____ **d.** shares of ownership in a company

_____ **e.** a crop that is sold for money

_____ **f.** a servant who serves someone, usually five to seven years, in exchange for something

_____ **g.** a lawmaking body that gave some Virginia colonists a voice in their government

_____ **h.** an agreement the Pilgrims wrote to make just laws and form a government for their colony

_____ **i.** a leader of a Native American people

©Macmillan/McGraw-Hill

Our Nation

Practice and Activity

Settling the New England Colonies

Each person shown below played a part in settling the New England colonies. Complete the statements about each person by filling in the blanks. For help, refer to pages 180 to 185 in your textbook.

1. I was the leader of the _____.

   Like the Pilgrims, we decided to leave

   _____ to practice our

   _____ in peace. We founded

   _____. We named

   our first settlement _____.

John Winthrop

2. I believed that Puritan leaders needed to _____

   different religious beliefs. I fled Massachusetts and

   founded the settlement of _____.

   Later it became the colony of _____.

   It was the first European colony to allow

   _____.

Roger Williams

3. My beliefs were different from those of

   _____. As a result, I was

   forced to leave_____.

   I traveled to _____ and

   started the settlement of _____.

Anne Hutchinson

© Macmillan/McGraw-Hill

Using an Elevation Map

Use the map to answer the questions below. For help, refer to pages 186 and 187 in your textbook.

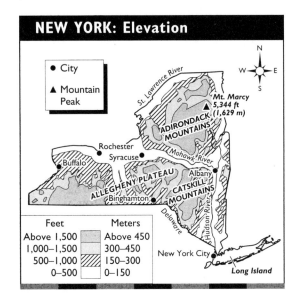

NEW YORK: Elevation

- • City
- ▲ Mountain Peak

Mt. Marcy
5,344 ft
(1,629 m)

ADIRONDACK MOUNTAINS

St. Lawrence River

Rochester
Syracuse
Buffalo

Mohawk River

ALLEGHENY PLATEAU

Binghamton

Albany

CATSKILL MOUNTAINS

Delaware

Hudson River

New York City

Long Island

Feet		Meters
Above 1,500		Above 450
1,000–1,500		300–450
500–1,000		150–300
0–500		0–150

1. What is the title of this map?

_____

_____

2. What is elevation?

_____

_____

3. How is elevation measured?

_____

_____

4. How is sea level measured?

_____

_____

5. If you were to travel from Albany to Binghamton, what type of land might you see? (Circle one)

  a. flat plains

  b. hills and mountains

6. What is the range of elevation in New York?

_____

7. What is the elevation of the following areas in feet?

Buffalo _____

Mt. Marcy _____

Albany _____

Rochester _____

Binghamton _____

Long Island _____

The Middle Colonies

Use the picture and quote below to complete the activity. For help, refer to pages 188 to 191 in your textbook.

I am very sensible of unkindness and injustice that hath been too much exercised toward you by the people of these parts of the world, but I am not such a man.

—*William Penn*

1. a. The picture shows William Penn meeting with a group of Native Americans who made their home in Pennsylvania. Who were they?

_____

b. What might they be discussing?

_____

2. William Penn spoke the words next to the picture. What did he mean?

_____

_____

_____

3. a. What did William Penn name the colony that he founded?

_____

b. What was the name of Penn's settlement?

_____

4. Why did William Penn establish a colony?

_____

_____

_____

5. List the three other Middle Colonies.

_____

_____

_____

6. How did respect and cooperation among various groups of immigrants help the Middle Colonies prosper?

_____

_____

_____

The Southern Colonies

Use the map to complete the activity.
For help, refer to pages 192 to 195
in your textbook.

1. Label the following Southern Colonies
   on the map.

   Maryland   North Carolina
   Georgia   Virginia
   South Carolina

2. Label the following settlements on
   the map.

   Baltimore   Charles Town
   Jamestown   Savannah

3. a. Which original Southern Colony
      was later divided into two colonies?

      _____

   b. What were the two colonies called?

      _____

      _____

4. Why was Maryland founded?

   _____

   _____

5. Why was Georgia founded? _____

   _____

6. What practice led to slavery in Georgia? _____

   _____

   _____

   _____

7. How did the geography of the Southern Colonies help the colonists?

   _____

   _____

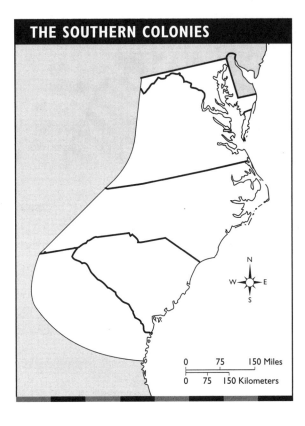

THE SOUTHERN COLONIES

0   75   150 Miles
0   75   150 Kilometers

Using New Words

Choose a word from the box to complete each sentence.
For help, refer to the lessons in Chapter 6 of your textbook.

cooperation	proprietor	tolerate
covenant	indigo	debtor
	confederacy	

1. If you owned land in a colony, you would be called a

   _____.

2. If you allow people to have beliefs different from your own, you

   _____ the differences.

3. If you were talking about a plant that produces a blue dye, you might be

   referring to _____.

4. _____ occurs when two or more groups work together.

5. If you owed money to another person, you would be a

   _____.

6. A special promise or agreement between a person and God is called a

   _____.

7. If you were part of a group of people who joined together for a common

   cause, you might be part of a _____.

Coming to the English Colonies

Use what each character says to complete the activity.
For help, refer to pages 200 to 203 in your textbook.

1. a. Why did this man leave Scotland and come to the English colonies?

_____

_____

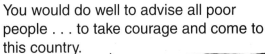

You would do well to advise all poor people . . . to take courage and come to this country.

b. List three things that the new colonies had to offer him.

_____

_____

_____

2. a. This woman was an indentured servant. Explain.

_____

_____

_____

_____

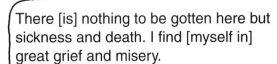

There [is] nothing to be gotten here but sickness and death. I find [myself in] great grief and misery.

b. What kind of "grief and misery" did this woman find in the colonies?

_____

_____

We were packed together in chains so tightly we could hardly move or turn over. . . . Many slaves fell sick and died.

3. a. This man from Africa was forced to come to the English colonies. Why?

_____

b. What is he describing?

_____

_____

©Macmillan/McGraw-Hill

My Life as a Colonist

Imagine you live on a farm in one of the English Colonies. Then read and answer the questions. Next use the space provided to write a diary entry. Write about a day in your life, including chores and schoolwork. For help, refer to pages 204 to 209 in your textbook.

1. For which farm chores are you responsible?

_____

_____

_____

2. Where, when, and by whom are you schooled?

_____

_____

_____

3. Are you satisfied with farming or would you like to learn a skill or craft? Explain.

_____

_____

_____

4. Which colonial city would you like to visit? Why?

_____

_____

_____

©Macmillan/McGraw-Hill

Thinking About Colonial Slavery

The picture below shows a newspaper advertisement that appeared in the 1700s. Use the ad to answer the questions. For help, refer to pages 210 to 215 in your textbook.

1. What is the ad announcing?

   _____

2. According to the ad, where were the Africans from?

   _____

   From which two present-day countries did most enslaved Africans come?

   _____

   _____

3. In which region of the English colonies would you expect to see this ad? Why?

> **GAMBIA NEGROES**
> TO BE SOLD
> On TUESDAY, the 7th of June
> On board the SHIP
> **MENTOR**
>
> A Cargo of 150 healthy young Negroes, just arrived from the river Gambia, after a passage of 35 days.
> The Negroes from this part of the coast of Africa are well acquainted with the cultivation of rice and are naturally industrious.
> **ROBERT HAZLEHURST & Co.**
> No. 44. Bay.

   _____

   _____

   _____

4. Why did this region have so many enslaved workers? _____

   _____

5. What gave many enslaved Africans reason to hope for freedom?

   _____

   _____

6. What effect did slavery have on the English colonies? _____

   _____

   _____

Looking at the Colonial Economy

Use the maps to complete the activity. For help, refer to pages 216 to 221 in your textbook.

1. a. Draw a line to the map of the Southern Colonies.

b. Why was this region well suited for growing crops?

_____

_____

c. Name three cash crops grown in this region for export.

_____

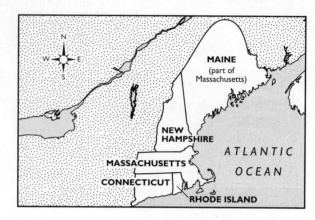

2. a. Draw a line to the map of the Middle Colonies.

b. Why was this region called the "breadbasket of the colonies"?

_____

_____

_____

c. Where did the farmers in this region sell their surplus grain?

_____

3. a. Draw a line to the map of the New England colonies.

b. Name two ways New Englanders made a living.

_____

c. List four places where New Englanders sold their products.

_____

_____

_____

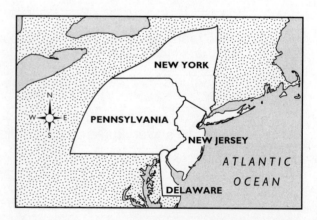

Write a Summary

Read the paragraph below. Then complete the activity.
For help, refer to pages 222 and 223 in your textbook.

By the middle of the 1700s the 13 colonies had a strong and growing economy. Some major industries included farming, fishing, shipbuilding, and trading. As the colonial economy grew, so did the colonists' ability to supply most needed goods at home. This ability lessened colonial reliance on goods imported from Britain. It also inspired the colonists to gain more control over their own economy. They soon began trading with nations other than England, a practice that defied British trade laws. Over the years, the colonists continued to rebel against British rule. Eventually, they would declare their independence from Great Britain.

1. Write the topic sentence.

_____

2. Write three important details that support the topic sentence.

_____

_____

3. Write a summary using the topic sentence and the details you recorded.

_____

_____

_____

©Macmillan/McGraw-Hill

Governing Colonial America

Write each statement from the box under the picture it fits. Then answer the questions. For help, refer to pages 224 to 229 in your textbook.

- chosen by the king of England
- body of delegates of white, Protestant, male landowners
- has the power to dissolve colonial assembly
- decides how the colonies will spend tax dollars
- George Washington a member
- enforces English laws in the colonies

Royal Governor

Colonial assemblies

1. _____

2. _____

3. _____

4. _____

5. _____

6. _____

7. What did the colonial delegates speak up for in their assemblies?

_____

8. Which important right did John Peter Zenger's trial establish in the colonies?

_____

©Macmillan/McGraw-Hill

Chapter 7 · pp. 224–229

Working with New Words

Write the letter of each term next to its meaning. For help, refer to the lessons in Chapter 7 of your textbook.

a. autobiography	**e.** export	**i.** slave trade	**m.** plantation
b. Middle Passage	**f.** frontier	**j.** agriculture	**n.** industry
c. free enterprise	**g.** militia	**k.** backcountry	**o.** overseer
d. triangular trade	**h.** assembly	**l.** slave codes	**p.** treason

_____ **1.** a large Southern farm

_____ **2.** the name the colonists gave to the foothills between the Appalachian Mountains and the Atlantic Coastal Plain

_____ **3.** a system in which any person can start a business and decide what to make, how much to produce, and what price to charge

_____ **4.** the business of buying and selling people for profit

_____ **5.** the triangular trade route's middle leg, which began in Africa and ended in the West Indies

_____ **6.** the business of farming

_____ **7.** the boss of a plantation

_____ **8.** betraying one's country by helping the enemy

_____ **9.** the story of a person's own life, written by himself or herself

_____ **10.** to send goods to other countries for sale or trade

_____ **11.** a trade route ranging from the colonies to Africa to the West Indies to the colonies

_____ **12.** a lawmaking body

_____ **13.** all the businesses that make one kind of product or provide one kind of service

_____ **14.** rules designed to keep enslaved workers under control

_____ **15.** the far edge of a country, where people are just beginning to settle

_____ **16.** a colonial military force made up of volunteers

New Spain and the Spanish Missions

Use the map to complete the activity below. For help, refer to pages 234 to 239 in your textbook.

NEW SPAIN IN THE 1700s

- ▲ Settlement
- + Mission
- — Present-day borders are shown

San Francisco
Monterey
Santa Fe
Rio Grande
San Antonio

PACIFIC OCEAN

Gulf of Mexico

N W E S

0 200 400 Miles
0 200 400 Kilometers

1. Label the following areas of New Spain on the map:
   Mexico   New Mexico
   California   Texas

2. Which parts of New Spain did El Camino Real connect?

   _____

   _____

   _____

3. Put an **X** on the city where the Alamo was located.

   To what does the Alamo Chain refer?

   _____

   _____

4. Locate and label the place in California where the first Spanish mission was founded. (San Diego)

5. What was the purpose of the mission?

   _____

   _____

   _____

6. Why did the Pueblo revolt against the Spanish?

   _____

   _____

   _____

Our Nation

Practice and Activity

The Builders of New France

Read the paragraphs below. Fill in the blanks to complete the activity. For help, refer to pages 240 to 243 in your textbook.

English	Gulf of Mexico	missionaries	New Orleans
trading posts	Louisiana	fur traders	Rene Robert La Salle
Chicago	Mississippi	Detroit	economic

In 1660, about 3,000 colonists lived in New France. Most were

_____ and _____.

The fur trade was the major source of _____

activity for the French. As the fur trade grew, a network of busy French

_____ spread throughout North America. One of

these grew into the city of _____, in Michigan.

Another became the city of _____, in Illinois.

In 1682, _____ followed the Mississippi River

to the _____. He claimed the entire

_____ Valley for France, naming it

_____. The capital of this territory,

_____, was established in 1722. The establishment

of French territory west of the 13 colonies prevented the _____

from expanding further.

©Macmillan/McGraw-Hill

Making Generalizations

Read the information in the Facts box. Then complete the activity.
For help, refer to pages 244 and 245 in your textbook.

FACTS
By 1660, 3,000 colonists lived in New France.
French colonists were not allowed to own land.
Most French colonists were fur traders or missionaries.
The French settlements were called trading posts.
By 1660, 75,000 colonists lived in the English colonies.
English colonists were allowed to own land.
Many English colonists became wealthy landowners.

1. Can you make a generalization based on the information in the Facts box? Check the best one.

    _____ **a.** Most English colonists became wealthy.

    _____ **b.** The majority of French colonists probably had some involvement in the fur trade.

    _____ **c.** New France had so few colonists because France prohibited land ownership.

    _____ **d.** French missionaries and fur traders got along well.

    _____ **e.** The French came to New France looking for land.

2. How did you decide on your answers to the first question?

    _____

    _____

    _____

    _____

3. Why is it useful to be able to make generalizations about a topic?

    _____

    _____

©Macmillan/McGraw-Hill

Our Nation

Practice and Activity

The Changing Face of North America

Use the maps to answer the questions. For help, refer to pages 246 to 249 in your textbook.

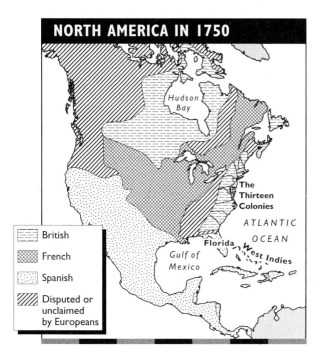

1. Which three nations are represented on the maps?

   _____

   _____

2. Which war took place between the dates on the two maps?

   _____

3. Which two nations fought against each other during this war?

   _____

4. What caused the war?

   _____

   _____

   _____

5. Which countries gained land between 1750 and 1763?

   _____

6. Which country lost land between 1750 and 1763?

   _____

7. As a result of this war, over which regions of North America did Britain gain control?

   _____

   _____

   _____

8. Which treaty guaranteed Britiain this territory?

   _____

Linking New Words and Ideas

Write a term from the box next to its definition. For help, refer to the lessons in Chapter 8 of your textbook.

mission	voyageur	Treaty of Paris	French and Indian War
presidio	coureur de bois	Proclamation of 1763	convert

_____

_____

_____

_____

_____

_____

_____

1. This is the name given the fighting in which the French and their Native American allies united against the British colonists.

2. This document, signed by Great Britain and France in 1763, officially ended the French and Indian War.

3. This means to cause a person to change a belief.

4. This document, issued by Great Britain, set aside all British lands west of the Appalachian Mountains for Native Americans.

5. This was a settlement where missionaries lived, worked, and tried to convert Native Americans to Christianity.

6. This term was used to describe a person who trapped furs without permission from the French government.

7. This word refers to a military fort where soldiers live.

8. This was a person in New France who transported furs and other goods from one trading post to the next by canoe.

Britain and the Colonies in Conflict

Read the sentences in the box. Then use them to make a chart showing
how conflict grew between the British and the colonists. (The first event
has been filled in for you.) Afterward, answer the questions. For help, refer
to pages 262 to 267 in your textbook.

- With the Intolerable Acts, Britain closes the port of Boston and bans town meetings.
- The Townshend Acts called for new taxes. The British demanded that the colonists pay taxes on products imported from Britain.
- The British Parliament passes the Stamp Act to collect more taxes from the colonies.
- Samuel Adams seeks to form Committees of Correspondence to "state the rights of the colonists."
- British soldiers kill five colonists during the Boston Massacre.
- The Boston Tea Party takes place to protest the British tax on tea.

DATE	EVENT
1765	The British Parliament passes the Stamp Act to collect taxes from the colonies.
1767	
1770	
1772	
1773	
1774	

1. How many years do the events in the chart cover? _____

2. Which event was the most important in uniting the colonists? Why?

_____

_____

_____

Reading a Political Cartoon

Use the political cartoon to complete the activity. For help, refer to pages 268 and 269 in your textbook.

Take back your trash!

1. What is a political cartoon? _____

_____

_____

2. What issue does the political cartoon shown here focus on?

_____

_____

3. Which image symbolizes Great Britain?

_____

Explain _____

_____

4. Which images symbolize the dissatisfaction of the colonists? _____

Explain _____

_____

5. Who are the people tossing the bags of trash? _____

Explain _____

_____

The American Revolution Begins

Use the map to complete the activity. For help, refer to pages 270 to 275 in your textbook.

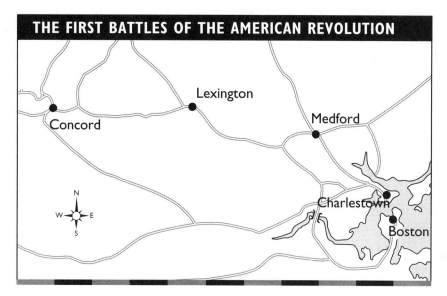

THE FIRST BATTLES OF THE AMERICAN REVOLUTION

1. Find the route Paul Revere took on the night of April 18, 1775. Trace it in blue.

   Why did Paul Revere make this ride?

   _____

   _____

   _____

2. Find where the first battle of the American Revolution was fought. Circle it in green.

3. Find where the British headed after the first battle of the American Revolution. Trace their route in red.

   What did the British do when they reached this site?

   _____

   _____

What was the outcome of this battle?

_____

_____

4. Identify two other military events that proved the colonists were serious in their struggle against the British.

   _____

   _____

   _____

5. What did colonial unity and military readiness in these early battles lay the groundwork for?

   _____

   _____

The Declaration of Independence

Thomas Jefferson, the author of the Declaration of Independence, called it "an expression of the American mind." Read this excerpt from the Declaration. Then answer the questions that follow. For help, refer to pages 276 to 283 in your textbook.

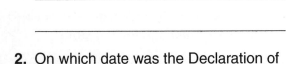

We hold these truths to be self-evident that all men are created equal, that they are endowed by their Creator with certain unalienable rights, that among these are life, liberty, and the pursuit of happiness.
    That to secure these rights, governments are instituted among men, deriving their just powers from the consent of the governed, that whenever any form of government becomes destructive of these ends, it is the right of the people to alter or to abolish it, and to institute new government, laying its foundation on such principles and organizing its powers in such form, as to them shall seem most likely to effect their safety and happiness.

1. Why was the Declaration of Independence written?

_____

_____

_____

2. On which date was the Declaration of Independence approved?

_____

3. What is the first truth mentioned in the Declaration of Independence?

_____

4. Which unalienable rights does the Declaration of Independence acknowledge?

_____

_____

5. What does the Declaration of Independence say people have the right to do when a government becomes destructive?

_____

_____

_____

6. Why is the Declaration of Independence one of the most important documents in the history of our nation?

_____

_____

_____

_____

_____

©Macmillan/McGraw-Hill

Matching Words and Their Meanings

Write the letter of the term that matches each definition. For help, refer
to the lessons in Chapter 9 of your textbook.

a. repeal	**e.** Declaration of	**h.** Intolerable Acts	**l.** minutemen
b. boycott	Independence	**i.** Patriot	**m.** militia
c. Continental army	**f.** traitor	**j.** Loyalist	
d. Boston Massacre	**g.** Townshend Acts	**k.** Stamp Act	

_____ **1.** a person who remained loyal to Britain during the Revolution

_____ **2.** a person who supported the colonists' fight for freedom

_____ **3.** one of the first British laws placing taxes on the colonies

_____ **4.** to cancel or take back

_____ **5.** laws that made colonists pay taxes on everyday items imported from Britain

_____ **6.** to refuse to do business or have contact with a person, group, or country

_____ **7.** someone who turns against his or her country

_____ **8.** a military force made up of volunteers

_____ **9.** the reaction of the British Parliament to the Boston Tea Party

_____ **10.** an army consisting of troops from every colony

_____ **11.** volunteer soldiers ready to defend the colonies at a minute's notice

_____ **12.** British soldiers kill five colonists during unrest in Boston as British troops entered the city

_____ **13.** a document explaining to the world why the colonies had to separate from Great Britain

Winning the War

Use the pictures to complete the activity. For help, refer to pages 288 to 293 in your textbook.

1. a. Draw a line to the person who sewed socks and cooked soup for the soldiers.

   b. In what other way did this person help the war effort?

_____

_____

_____

_____

Martha Washington

2. a. Draw a line to the person who became the Commander-in-Chief of the Continental army.

   b. What was the name of one of the Commander's spy rings?

_____

   c. How did his policy toward enslaved blacks change during the war?

_____

_____

_____

Mary Ludwig Hays

3. a. Draw a line to the person who helped American soldiers on the battlefield.

   b. How did she help?

_____

_____

_____

   c. Who were two other women who helped the American cause?

_____

George Washington

From Defeat to Victory

Use the map to complete the activity. For help, refer to pages 294 to 299 in your textbook.

1. Circle Trenton on the map.

   How was the battle of Trenton won?

   _____

   _____

   _____

   _____

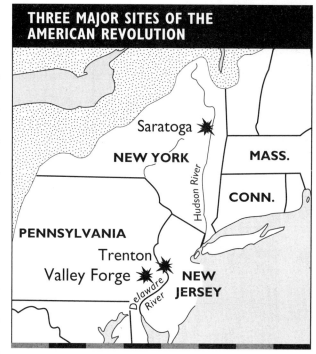

THREE MAJOR SITES OF THE AMERICAN REVOLUTION

   Circle Saratoga.

   Why was the battle at Saratoga a turning point in the war?

   _____

   _____

   _____

   Who led the Continental army during these battles? _____

2. Circle Valley Forge.

   What happened to the American troops during their winter at Valley Forge?

   _____

3. Who captured the Ohio River Valley? _____

   How did he outwit the British?

   _____

   _____

   _____

4. How did Captain John Paul Jones respond when the British asked if he were ready to surrender?

   _____

The War Ends

Read each statement. Then identify the mystery person. For help, refer to pages 300 to 305 in your textbook.

1. He opened the port of New Orleans to American ships.

_____

What other action did he take to aid the patriots in their

fight against Britain? _____

_____

2. They called this patriot the "Swamp Fox."

_____

How did he get the name "Swamp Fox"?

_____

_____

Who wrote a poem about this hero?

_____

3. Who said, "We fight, we get beat, rise and fight again"?

_____

What role did he play in the Revolution? _____

_____

4. Who said that he was "quite tired of marching about the country" chasing

Nathanael Greene? _____

What role did he play in the Revolution? _____

5. At war's end, who was quoted as saying that there were two revolutions?
One was the war itself. The other "was in the minds and hearts of the people."

_____

How might you interpret this statement? _____

_____

Comparing Maps at Different Scales

Use the maps below to complete the activity.
For help, refer to pages 306 and 307 in
your textbook.

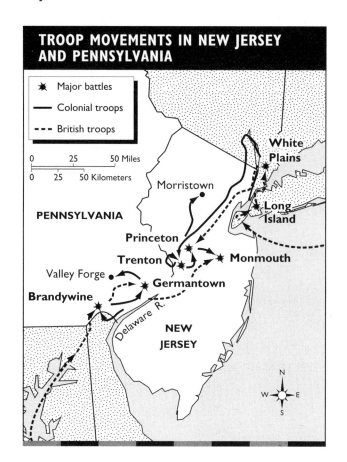

TROOP MOVEMENTS IN NEW JERSEY AND PENNSYLVANIA

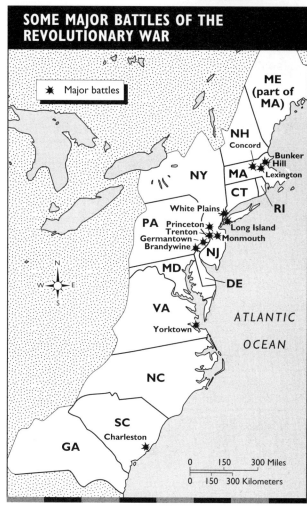

SOME MAJOR BATTLES OF THE REVOLUTIONARY WAR

1. How many colonies are shown on the small-scale map? _____

   How many colonies are shown on the large-scale map? _____

2. Which map shows the direction in which colonial troops moved through

   New Jersey? _____

3. What does the large-scale map show that the small-scale map does not?

   _____

4. Suppose you were Washington planning a battle strategy in the Middle Colonies.
   Which map would you use? Why?

   _____

Linking New Words and Ideas

Write each term from the box next to the sentence that defines it.
For help, refer to the lessons in Chapter 10 of your textbook.

mercenary	Treaty of Paris	Treaty of Alliance
surveyor	Second Treaty of Fort Stanwix	

_____

_____

_____

_____

_____

1. This settlement took land in the Ohio River Valley away from the Iroquois Confederacy.

2. You would hire this person to measure land.

3. This is a soldier who is paid to fight for another country.

4. After the Continental army's victory at Saratoga, the French showed their support for the patriots by signing this treaty.

5. In this 1783 document the British recognized the independence of the United States.

©Macmillan/McGraw-Hill

The Articles of Confederation

Read the statements carefully. Label each statement **T**rue or **F**alse.
Then write the reason for your answer. For help, refer to pages 312 to 315
in your textbook.

1. The cartoon shows one major weakness
   of the Articles of Confederation.

   _____

   _____

   _____

   _____

2. The Articles provided Congress with the
   power it needed to run the government.

   _____

   _____

3. Under the Articles of Confederation the states set up their own system of government.

   _____

   _____

   _____

4. The Articles made it easy for Congress to resolve conflicts between the states.

   _____

   _____

5. Shays's Rebellion was dismissed as an unimportant, though sad incident.

   _____

   _____

6. The Congress of the Confederation passed the Northwest Ordinance, an important law.

   _____

   _____

   _____

Planning a New Government

Think about what happened at the Constitutional Convention. Then complete
the activity. For help, refer to pages 316 to 321 in your textbook.

1. Describe the two conflicting proposals for establishing Congress.

   Virginia Plan: _____

   _____

   New Jersey Plan: _____

   _____

2. What was the "Great Compromise"?

   _____

   _____

   _____

   _____

3. Who proposed the compromise? _____

4. Describe two other compromises worked out during the Constitutional Convention.

   _____

   _____

   _____

5. Complete the chart below by describing the responsibilities of each branch of the new
   government.

BRANCH OF GOVERNMENT	RESPONSIBILITY
Legislative	
Executive	
Judicial	

©Macmillan/McGraw-Hill

Name: _____   Date: _____

Our Nation

Practice and Activity

Recognizing Point of View

Read each person's statement about the Constitution. Then read each question and circle the letter next to the correct answer. For help, refer to pages 322 and 323 in your textbook.

> My political curiosity . . . leads me to ask: Who authorized them to speak the language of *We the people*, instead of, *We the states*? . . . The federal Convention ought [only] to have amended the old system; for this purpose they were solely delegated.

> Sir, I agree with this Constitution with all its faults, if they are such; because I think a general government necessary for us. . . . I doubt too whether any other Convention we can obtain may be able to make a better Constitution.

Patrick Henry

Benjamin Franklin

1. Identify Patrick Henry's point of view.

   a. He felt the Constitutional Convention should have amended the old form of government instead of creating a new one.

   b. He felt that the Constitution was well-written and established a superior form of government.

   c. He felt that the Constitution should have been written differently, leaving out the words "We the people."

2. Identify Benjamin Franklin's point of view.

   a. He felt that a new Convention should be assembled to write another Constitution.

   b. He supported the Constitution even though it wasn't perfect. He felt that a new convention could not produce a better one.

   c. He felt that the Constitution had many faults and should not be supported by anyone.

3. Why is it important to recognize a person's point of view?

   _____

   _____

©Macmillan/McGraw-Hill

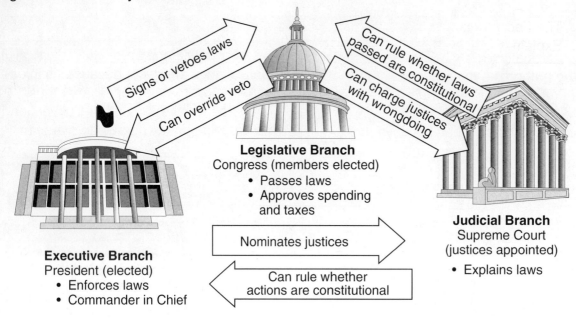

Name: _____ Date: _____

Thinking About the Constitution

Read the chart. Then complete each item below. For help, refer to pages 324 to 327 in your textbook.

Signs or vetoes laws

Can override veto

Can rule whether laws passed are constitutional

Can charge justices with wrongdoing

Legislative Branch
Congress (members elected)
• Passes laws
• Approves spending and taxes

Judicial Branch
Supreme Court (justices appointed)
• Explains laws

Nominates justices

Can rule whether actions are constitutional

Executive Branch
President (elected)
• Enforces laws
• Commander in Chief

1. Why did the authors of the Constitution set up the system of checks and balances?

_____

_____

2. How does this system affect the branches of government?

_____

_____

3. Study the chart and review Lesson 3 in your textbook. Then circle the sentences that state how our system of government works.

The President can order the army into battle, but only Congress can declare war.

Congress has the power to appoint the President.

The President can veto laws passed by Congress.

The Supreme Court can stop a law passed by Congress or signed by the President.

4. What system of government did the Constitution set up? _____

How does this system share power? _____

_____

Name: _____ Date: _____

Ratifying the Constitution

Complete the activities on this page. For help, refer to pages 328 to 333 in your textbook.

1. The Federalists and the Antifederalists disagreed about the Constitution. Explain each side's point of view in the space provided.

FEDERALISTS	ANTIFEDERALISTS

2. a. How did James Madison, Alexander Hamilton, and John Jay try to persuade reluctant states to ratify the Constitution?

_____

b. What role did John Hancock play in the ongoing debate? _____

_____

_____

3. How did Congress appease the Antifederalists?

_____

4. To help the President run the government, Congress set up a Cabinet. Each Cabinet position has a leader. Complete the chart by describing the responsibilities of each cabinet position.

CABINET POSITION	RESPONSIBILITY
Treasury	
State	
War	
Attorney General	

©Macmillan/McGraw-Hill

Matching Terms and Meanings

Write the letter of each term on the line in front of the term's definition.
For help, refer to the lessons in Chapter 11 of your textbook.

a. veto	**f.** Shay's Rebellion	**k.** executive branch	**p.** judicial branch
b. Virginia Plan	**g.** statehood	**l.** Antifederalists	**q.** political party
c. preamble	**h.** Articles of Confederation	**m.** Supreme Court	**r.** amendment
d. Cabinet	**i.** legislative branch	**n.** Great Compromise	**s.** federal system
e. Federalists	**j.** New Jersey Plan	**o.** checks and balances	**t.** Bill of Rights

_____ **1.** the document that set up our country's first central government

_____ **2.** to become a state

_____ **3.** the lawmaking branch of government

_____ **4.** the branch of government that carries out the laws made by Congress

_____ **5.** the branch of government that decides the meaning of the laws

_____ **6.** the head of the judicial branch of government

_____ **7.** a plan that gave small and large states an equal number of representatives

_____ **8.** a proposal that Congress should have two separate houses, one based on state population and the other based on equal state representation

_____ **9.** called for one house of Congress based on population

_____ **10.** farmers protest the land tax imposed by Massachusetts

_____ **11.** an addition to a constitution or other document

_____ **12.** an introduction to a document

_____ **13.** a system in which the states and the federal government share power

_____ **14.** a system in which one branch of government is balanced by another

_____ **15.** to refuse to approve

_____ **16.** supporters of the ratification of the Constitution

_____ **17.** opponents of the ratification of the Constitution

_____ **18.** a document that describes the basic rights of people

_____ **19.** a government body made up of secretaries of departments

_____ **20.** a group of people who share similar ideas about government

West of the Appalachians

Use the map to help you complete the activity. For additional help, refer to pages 346 to 349 in your textbook.

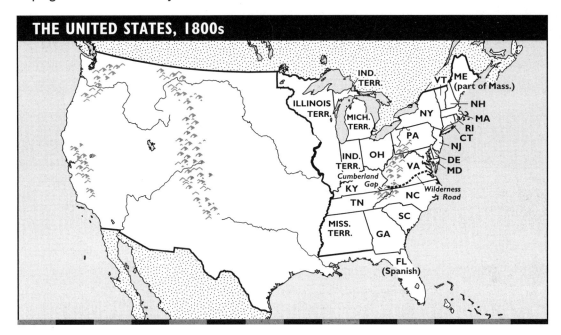

THE UNITED STATES, 1800s

1. Which mountain range did pioneers cross in search of land out west?

   _____

   Label this mountain range on the map.

2. Label the Mississippi River. Trace its route in blue.

3. Label the Central Plains and the Gulf Coastal Plain.

   Why did the pioneers leave the East to settle on these plains?

   _____

   _____

   _____

   _____

4. How did trailblazers help make westward travel easier for pioneers?

   _____

   _____

   _____

   _____

5. Find the Cumberland Gap. What famous trailblazer crossed the gap to settle in Kentucky?

   _____

6. Why was the Wilderness Road

   important? _____

   _____

   _____

Jefferson in the News

The headlines at right could have appeared in United States newspapers during the early 1800s. Read each headline and answer the questions. For help, refer to pages 350 to 355 in your textbook.

1. a. In which year would this headline have appeared?

_____

b. What was Jefferson's view on the best kind of government?

_____

_____

c. Which European country did Jefferson believe threatened the United States?

_____

> ## Jefferson Becomes President
>
> **Today, Thomas Jefferson began his duties as President of the United States.**

2. a. In which year would this headline have appeared?

_____

b. What was this land deal later called?

_____

c. What land did the United States acquire?

_____

_____

> ## U.S. and France Make Land Deal
>
> **President Jefferson announced today that the United States had reached an agreement with France.**

3. a. In which year would this headline have appeared?

_____

b. What did Lewis and Clark want to accomplish?

_____

_____

c. What Native American helped them?

_____

> ## Lewis and Clark Reach Goal
>
> **Eighteen months after they set out to explore the Louisiana Territory, Lewis and Clark finally reached their goal.**

Comparing Maps

Use the maps to complete the activity. For help, refer to
pages 356 and 357 in your textbook.

MAP A: BATTLES OF THE WAR OF 1812

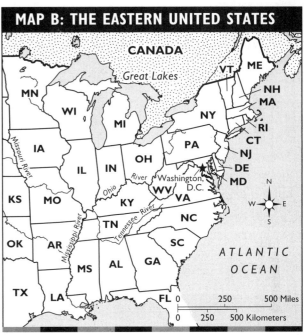

MAP B: THE EASTERN UNITED STATES

1. What kind of map is Map A?

   political   relief   historical

2. What kind of map is Map B?

   political   relief   historical

3. In which present-day state did the
   battle of Horseshoe Bend take place?

   _____

   How did you find the answer?

   _____

   _____

   _____

   _____

4. Locate the states of Wisconsin and
   Illinois on Map B. What was this area
   during the War of 1812?

   _____

   How did you find the answer?

   _____

   _____

5. Which maps would you compare to
   discover which battles of the War of
   1812 were fought in the mountains?

   political and relief

   relief and historical

   historical and political

Events in the War of 1812

The excerpt was written by Isaac Hull, captain of the USS *Constitution,* after a battle. Read the excerpt and then answer the questions. For help, refer to pages 358 to 363 in your textbook.

After informing you that so fine a ship as the *Guerrière* . . . had been totally . . . cut to pieces so as to make her not worth towing into port . . . you can have no doubt of the gallantry and good conduct of the officers and ship's company I have the honor to command. It only remains, therefore, for me to assure you that they all fought with great bravery.

—Isaac Hull

Richard Morris and James Woodress, editors, *Voices from America's Past* (New York: E. P. Dutton, 1963).

1. Under which flag did the *Guerrière* sail?

   _____

2. What happened to the *Guerrière*?

   _____

   _____

3. During which war was the letter written?

   _____

4. Which nations were at war?

   _____

   _____

5. What caused the war?

   _____

   _____

   _____

6. The land war was more difficult for the United States than the war at sea. Why?

   _____

   _____

   _____

   _____

7. What was the Monroe Doctrine?

   _____

   _____

   _____

8. What promise did the Monroe Doctrine offer European nations?

   _____

   _____

   _____

©Macmillan/McGraw-Hill

Our Nation

Practice and Activity

Thinking About New Words

Write each word or term from the box under the phrase that defines it.
For help, you can refer to the lessons in Chapter 12 of your textbook.

pioneer	Louisiana Purchase	War of 1812
neutral	Era of Good Feelings	
War Hawks	Monroe Doctrine	

1. a warning made by James Monroe to Europe. Monroe said the U.S. opposed future colonization in the Western Hemisphere.

_____

2. a person who leads the way into new areas

_____

3. the land west of the Mississippi River that the United States purchased from France in 1803

_____

4. a period of peace and prosperity for the United States that began at the end of the War of 1812

_____

5. not taking sides on an issue

_____

6. during Madison's presidency, members of Congress who wanted to declare war against Great Britain

_____

7. a conflict between Great Britain and the United States that began because Great Britain started taking American ships and sailors

_____

©Macmillan/McGraw-Hill

From Producer to Consumer

Study the drawings below. Then describe what is happening in each step in the production of a cotton dress.

1.

_____

_____

_____

_____

2.

_____

_____

_____

_____

3.

_____

_____

_____

_____

4.

_____

_____

_____

_____

Andrew Jackson's Presidency

Answer the question to complete the activity. For help, refer to pages 376 to 381 in your textbook.

1. The poster refers to Jackson as "Old Hickory." Why was he given this nickname?

_____

_____

_____

_____

2. In what kind of government did

Jackson believe? _____

_____

_____

3. How did voting laws in states new to the Union help Jackson get elected?

_____

_____

_____

_____

4. What was one outcome of Jackson's quarrel with the Bank of the United States?

_____

_____

_____

_____

5. Describe Jackson's views on Native Americans. What happened as a result?

_____

_____

_____

Name: _____ Date: _____

Identifying Western Trails

Use the map to complete the activity. For help, refer to pages 384 to 389 in your textbook.

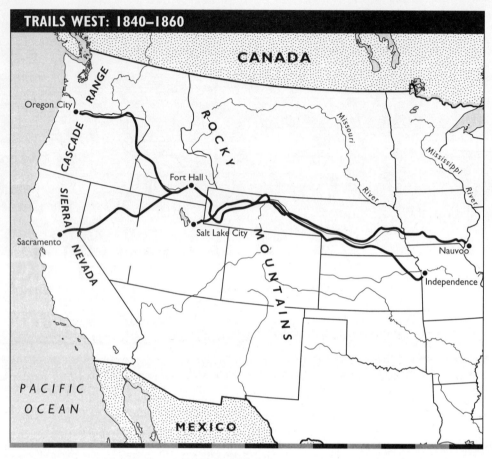

TRAILS WEST: 1840–1860

CANADA

Oregon City

CASCADE RANGE

ROCKY

Missouri

Mississippi River

Fort Hall

SIERRA NEVADA

Salt Lake City

MOUNTAINS

Sacramento

Nauvoo

Independence

PACIFIC OCEAN

MEXICO

1. a. Label the Oregon Trail. Trace its route in green.

   b. Why did large numbers of people travel this trail? _____

   _____

   _____

2. a. Label the Mormon Trail. Trace its route in brown.

   b. How did this trail get its name? _____

   _____

3. a. Label the California Trail. Trace its route in red.

   b. What event caused large numbers of people to travel across this trail?

   _____

Telling Fact from Opinion

The paragraph was taken from Lesson 3, page 384. Read the paragraph. Then follow the directions to complete the activity. For help, refer to pages 390 and 391 in your textbook.

We left our home in Iowa with three wagons drawn by seven yoke [pairs] of oxen, it was thought that horses were not suitable to draw wagons across the Rocky Mountains. . . . Two of the wagons were loaded with provisions [supplies] and the third a light wagon carried the small children and some beds.

—This is how John Breen recalled his family's move to the West in 1846. Breen was one of thousands of people who traveled to the West to begin a new life.

1. Underline the sentences in the paragraph that state facts. Explain how you determined the factual statements.

   _____

   _____

   _____

2. List the opinion stated in the paragraph. Do you think it was based on some truth? Explain your answer.

   _____

   _____

   _____

3. Did you find any clue words in the opinion statement? List them.

   _____

A Chart of Texas History

Use the information in the box to complete the chart of Texas history. Then answer the questions below. For help, refer to pages 392 to 399 in your textbook.

> - Stephen Austin leads 300 American families to settle in Texas.
> - Mexican soldiers defeat the Texas army at The Alamo.
> - The Mexican government jails Stephen Austin.
> - Mexican leaders stop all immigration from the United States.
> - Texas becomes the 28th state of the United States.
> - Mexico, which includes Texas, wins independence from Spain.
> - Santa Anna grants Texas its independence.

DATE	EVENT
1821	Mexico, which includes Texas, wins independence from Spain.
1822	
1830	
1833	
March 1836	
April 1836	
1845	

1. For how many years was Texas a part of Mexico? _____

2. How many years passed from the time Mexico won independence from Spain until

   Texas won statehood? _____

3. Why was statehood denied Texas for many years? _____

   _____

   _____

   _____

Linking New Words and Ideas

Write each word or term from the box next to the sentence that tells about it. For help, refer to the lessons in Chapter 13 of your textbook.

steam engine	reaper	cotton gin	manifest destiny	canal
wagon train	Mountain Man	forty-niners	Indian Removal Act	Gold Rush
Industrial Revolution		interchangeable parts		Treaty of Guadalupe Hidalgo

_____ 1. a law allowing the President to remove Native Americans from their homeland and relocate them to Indian Territory

_____ 2. a large group of wagons carrying settlers west

_____ 3. fur trappers living in the western mountains

_____ 4. when large numbers of people went to California seeking gold

_____ 5. standard-size parts which allowed replacement of damaged parts in a manufactured item

_____ 6. a machine used to remove seeds from cotton

_____ 7. an engine using steam for power

_____ 8. a period in which goods that had been made by hand were now made by machines, often in factories

_____ 9. a human-built waterway

_____ 10. searched for gold in California in 1849

_____ 11. uses sharp blades to cut and harvest grain

_____ 12. ended the Mexican War

_____ 13. the idea that the United States was to claim for itself all the land from the Atlantic to the Pacific oceans

©Macmillan/McGraw-Hill

Comparing Sides on Slavery

The maps below show how the country was divided on slavery. Circle the name of the region that each sentence describes. For help, refer to pages 410 to 415 in your textbook.

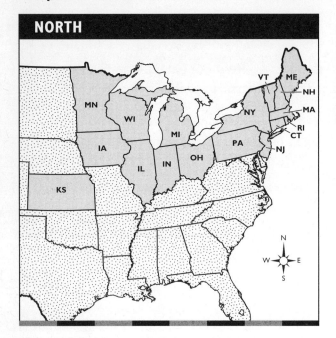

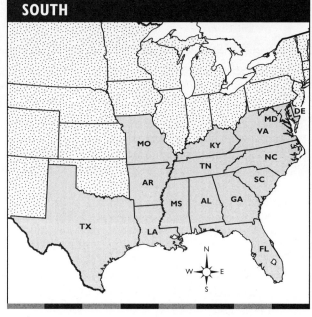

1. This region had become wealthy because of cotton grown on large plantations.

   North   South

2. Manufacturing was becoming much more important in this region's economy.

   North   South

3. Thousands of immigrants were settling in this region's cities, where jobs were plentiful.

   North   South

4. About four million enslaved Africans were forced to work on the cotton plantations in this region.

   North   South

5. Merchants in this region made money shipping cotton.

   North   South

6. Most states in this region had ended slavery.

   North   South

7. A number of slave rebellions took place in this region.

   North   South

8. Even though most states in this region had ended slavery, there was much prejudice against Africans.

   North   South

©Macmillan/McGraw-Hill

People Fighting for Equality

Use the pictures on the right to complete the activity. Write the number of each statement on the line next to the person it describes. For help, refer to pages 416 to 421 in your textbook.

1. This person started a newspaper called *The Liberator*. He believed that slavery was wrong and should be ended.

_____

Lucretia Mott and Elizabeth Cady Stanton

2. These sisters, daughters of a plantation owner, were among the first women to speak publicly for the abolitionist cause.

_____

William Lloyd Garrison

3. This former slave became the most famous conductor on the Underground Railroad.

4. These women organized the Seneca Falls Convention, the first convention to discuss the rights of women.

_____

Sojourner Truth

5. This former slave traveled the country giving speeches in support of abolition and women's rights.

_____

Harriet Tubman

_____

Sara and Angelina Grimké

Reading a Newspaper

The article below might have appeared in a newspaper in 1831. Read the article. Then complete the activity. For help, refer to pages 422 and 423 in your textbook.

Garrison Publishes Abolitionist Newspaper

Boston, Massachusetts, January 2, 1831

In Boston yesterday Mr. William Lloyd Garrison began publication of his newspaper, *The Liberator.* The paper promises to encourage the abolitionist cause.

In a front page editorial, Garrison argued for the immediate freedom of all slaves! He also promised that *The Liberator* would stir the conscience of the nation as never before.

Reaction in some parts of the South has been extreme. Many Southern leaders have demanded that Garrison be jailed. Some have even gone as far as offering a reward for his kidnapping. Already jailed once for his abolitionist views, Garrison seems unaffected by these threats and remains steadfast in his commitment to the abolitionist cause.

1. Circle the headline. What does the headline tell you?

   _____

   _____

2. Underline the dateline. What does a dateline tell you?

   _____

   _____

3. The article gives facts about a recent event. What kind of article is it?

   _____

4. What is the article about?

   _____

   _____

5. When and where did the event described in the article take place?

   _____

   _____

6. Where in the newspaper would you look to find the editor's opinion about the event or article?

   _____

©Macmillan/McGraw-Hill

Charting Events Leading to War

Use the events in the box to complete the Event column in the chart. Then fill
in the Result column. Some events and their results have been filled in for you.
For help, refer to pages 424 to 429 in your textbook.

> - The Confederate States of America was formed.
> - The Compromise of 1850 was approved.
> - Congress passed the Kansas-Nebraska Act.
> - John Brown raided Harpers Ferry.
> - The Supreme Court made the Dred Scott Decision.
> - Lincoln was elected President.

EVENTS LEADING TO WAR		
DATE	EVENT	RESULT
1850	The Compromise of 1850 was approved.	California was admitted to the Union as a free state. In return, the North accepted the Fugitive Slave Law, which called for the North to help capture escaped slaves.
1854		Kansas and Nebraska were allowed to decide for themselves whether to allow slavery.
1857	The Supreme Court made the Dred Scott Decision.	
1859		This raid deepened tensions between the North and the South.
1860	Lincoln was elected President.	
1861		The Union was split apart.

©Macmillan/McGraw-Hill

Using New Words

Write each term in the box under the matching definition.
For help, refer to the lessons in Chapter 14 of your textbook.

secede	Compromise of 1850	Kansas-Nebraska Act
abolitionist	Dred Scott Decision	Seneca Falls Convention
states' rights	Fugitive Slave Law	Underground Railroad
the Confederacy	prejudice	Missouri Compromise

1. said slaves were property

_____

2. used to refer to a state's leaving the Union

_____

3. the name of the first convention held to discuss the rights of women

_____

4. the name of the compromise that divided the United States into free states and slave states

_____

5. the name of the new country formed by the states that had seceded from the Union

_____

6. the name of the compromise that allowed California to be admitted to the United States as a free state

_____

7. allowed Kansas and Nebraska to decide for themselves whether or not to allow slavery

_____

8. someone who wanted to end slavery in the United States

_____

9. the idea that each state should be allowed to make its own decisions about most issues

_____

10. the system of secret routes that escaping slaves followed to freedom

_____

11. required police in free states to help capture escaping slaves

_____

12. a negative opinion formed without proof

_____

©Macmillan/McGraw-Hill

The Civil War Begins

Use the map below to complete the activity. For help, refer to
pages 434 to 439 in your textbook.

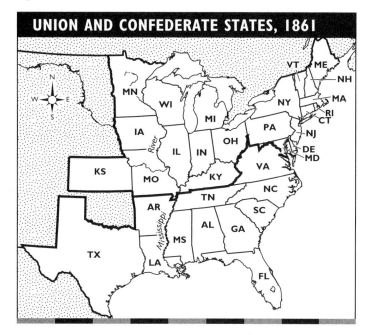

UNION AND CONFEDERATE STATES, 1861

1. Color the Union states on the map blue. Color the Confederate states gray.

2. What were the three parts of the Union's Anaconda Plan for victory?

   _____

   _____

   _____

3. Locate and label the site of the first battle of the Civil War. What caused the battle?

   _____

   _____

   _____

4. Locate and label the site of the First Battle of Bull Run. List two things this battle made
   people realize about the war.

   _____

   _____

   _____

Using a Population Distribution Map

Study the map and complete the chart below. (The first one is done for you.)
Then answer the questions by circling your answer. For help, refer to
pages 440 and 441 in your textbook.

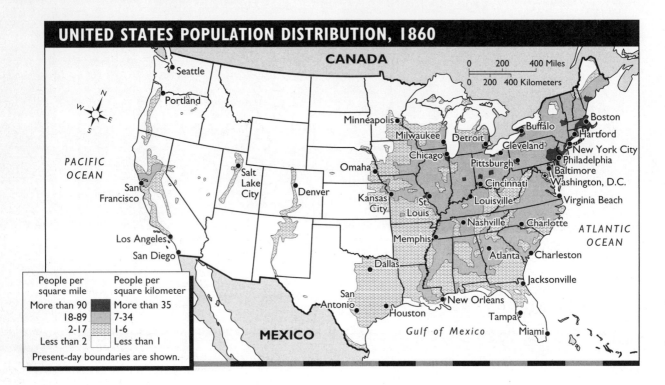

UNITED STATES POPULATION DISTRIBUTION, 1860

City	People Per Square Mile
Boston	more than 90
Charleston	
Chicago	
Dallas	
Denver	
New York	
Pittsburgh	
Seattle	
St. Louis	

1. Which area has the most people?

   Northeast   Southeast   Midwest

2. Which city has the fewest people?

   Boston   Nashville   Jacksonville

3. Which city has the most people?

   Pittsburgh   Omaha   Minneapolis

©Macmillan/McGraw-Hill

Name: _____   Date: _____

The War Takes a New Direction

Use the speeches at right to complete the activity. For help, refer to pages 442 to 447 in your textbook.

1. What is the name of the document this excerpt is from?

_____

_____

2. What two things did this document do?

_____

_____

_____

_____

_____

> *. . . all persons held as slaves within any state . . .*
> *in rebellion against the United States, shall be then, henceforth, and forever free.*

3. How did this document change the way people felt about the war?

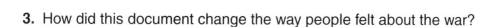

_____

_____

4. Read these words from a famous speech made by President Lincoln. Which battle is he referring to?

_____

5. How did this battle affect the course of the war?

_____

_____

_____

_____

> *Now we are engaged in a great civil war, testing whether that nation, or any nation so conceived, and so dedicated, can long endure. We are met on a great battlefield of that war. We have come to dedicate a portion of that field, as a final resting-place for those who here gave their lives, that that nation might live. It is altogether fitting and proper that we should do this.*

6. What did President Lincoln's speech make clear about the war?

_____

_____

©Macmillan / McGraw - Hill

Name: _____ Date: _____

The Civil War Ends

Use the map to help you complete the activity below. For help, refer
to pages 448 to 453 in your textbook.

MAJOR CIVIL WAR BATTLES

	Major battles
	Confederate states
	Union states, territories

1. Draw in red the route General Sherman
   took on his march through Georgia.

2. What did Grant order Sherman to do?

   _____

   _____

3. Circle the two cities on the map that
   Grant's men entered and captured.

4. Why had General Lee left these cities?

   _____

   _____

   _____

5. Put an **X** on the place where Lee
   surrendered to Grant.

   Why did Lee surrender?

   _____

   _____

   _____

   _____

6. How had the war changed the South?

   _____

   _____

   _____

   _____

Chapter 15 · pp. 448–453

Our Nation

Practice and Activity

Drawing Inferences

An inference is something you figure out based on clues and on information you already know. Read the passage below. Then answer the questions. For help, refer to pages 454 and 455 in your textbook.

> At the turn of the 20th century, two-thirds of the African Americans living in the South farmed land they did not own. Landlords provided these farmers, called *sharecroppers,* with seeds, food, clothing, and shelter. The sharecroppers repaid their landlords at the end of the harvest. After repaying their landlords, most sharecroppers wound up with very little earnings. Sometimes they even found themselves owing money at the end of the year.

1. What clues does the passage offer about the life of a sharecropper?

_____

_____

_____

2. How does the information compare with what you have read about the lives of African American sharecroppers?

_____

_____

_____

3. What inference can you draw about the future of sharecropping?

_____

_____

_____

_____

©Macmillan/McGraw-Hill

Thinking About Reconstruction

Read the statements below and label them **True** or **False.** Then write the reasons for your answer. For help, refer to pages 456 to 461 in your textbook.

1. The Fourteenth and Fifteenth amendments extended the rights of African Americans.

   _____

   _____

   _____

   _____

2. President Johnson carried out a plan for Reconstruction in the South. _____

   _____

   _____

3. Congress wanted President Johnson to end Reconstruction. _____

   _____

   _____

   _____

   _____

   _____

4. Congress created the Freedmen's Bureau to help African Americans after the Civil War.

   _____

   _____

5. Under Reconstruction, African American men were not able to vote. _____

   _____

   _____

6. When Reconstruction ended, the Southern states passed Jim Crow laws to help African Americans.

   _____

   _____

Our Nation

Practice and Activity

Matching Words and Their Meanings

Write the letter of each term next to its meaning. For help, refer to the lessons in Chapter 15 of your textbook.

a. total war	**f.** segregation	**j.** Freedmen's Bureau	**n.** Thirteenth Amendment
b. blockade	**g.** sharecropping	**k.** Anaconda Plan	**o.** Fourteenth Amendment
c. impeach	**h.** Jim Crow laws	**l.** Reconstruction	**p.** Emancipation Proclamation
d. Civil War	**i.** draft	**m.** Gettysburg Address	**q.** Fifteenth Amendment
e. black codes			**r.** civilian

_____ 1. the system of renting land for a share of the crop raised on the land

_____ 2. abolishes slavery

_____ 3. to block off

_____ 4. Southern laws that described the rights and duties of freed blacks

_____ 5. the announcement that ended slavery in the Confederacy

_____ 6. the separation of white people and black people

_____ 7. the selection of men who have to serve in the military

_____ 8. a famous speech by President Lincoln

_____ 9. gives all male citizens of the United States the right to vote, regardless of race

_____ 10. rebuilding the South

_____ 11. the Union's plan for victory in the Civil War

_____ 12. an agency established by Congress to help African Americans after the Civil War

_____ 13. the war between the Southern states and the Northern states

_____ 14. makes blacks citizens of the United States and guarantees them the same legal rights as whites

_____ 15. to charge a government official with wrongdoing

_____ 16. an all-out war to destroy people's ability and will to fight

_____ 17. a person not in the armed forces

_____ 18. laws that made discrimination against black people legal

©Macmillan/McGraw-Hill

The Transcontinental Railroad

Use the map to help you complete the activity. For help, refer to pages 474 to 479 in your textbook.

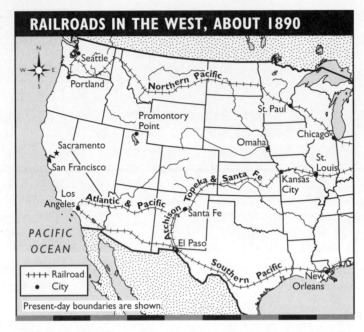

RAILROADS IN THE WEST, ABOUT 1890

1. Circle the two cities where construction on the transcontinental railroad began.

2. Put an **X** over the spot where the Union Pacific met the Central Pacific.

3. Draw the part of the railroad built by each company. Label each railroad line.

4. How did the workforces of the Central Pacific and the Union Pacific differ?

_____

_____

5. List a serious cost of building the transcontinental railroad.

_____

6. What happened to allow the building of a transcontinental railroad?

_____

_____

©Macmillan/McGraw-Hill

Chapter 16 · pp. 474–479

Reading Time Zone Maps

Use the time zone map below to complete the activity. For help, refer
to pages 480 and 481 in your textbook.

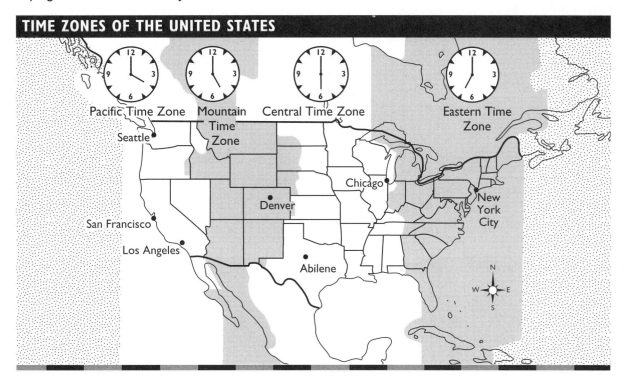

TIME ZONES OF THE UNITED STATES

Pacific Time Zone   Mountain Time Zone   Central Time Zone   Eastern Time Zone

Seattle

San Francisco

Los Angeles

Denver

Abilene

Chicago

New York City

1. How many time zones are shown on the map above?

_____

2. Find Abilene on the map. What time zone is it in?

_____

3. Find Los Angeles on the map. What time zone is it in?

_____

4. Which time zone do you live in?

_____

5. As you move from east to west, do you add or subtract an hour for each time zone that you cross?

_____

6. As you move from west to east, do you add or subtract an hour for each time zone that you cross?

_____

7. Use the time zone map above to complete the statements below.

   a. When it is 6:00 P.M. in New York City, it is _____ in San Francisco.

   b. When it is 2:00 P.M. in Chicago, it is _____ in Denver.

   c. When it is 9:00 A.M. in Seattle, it is _____ in Los Angeles.

Singing About Life on the Range

The song below was a favorite among cowboys during the era of cattle drives. Use the song to complete the activity. For help, refer to pages 482 to 485 in your textbook.

THE OLD CHISHOLM TRAIL

Moderately

Well, come a-long boys and lis-ten to my tale, I'll tell you of my trou-bles on the old Chis-holm Trail. Come a ti yi yip-pi yip-pi yay yip-pi yay, Come a ti yi yip-pi yip — pi yay.

*A two-dollar horse and a forty-dollar saddle,
I'm gonna get punchin' those old Texas cattle.
Come a ti, etc.*

*It's cloudy in the west and it looks like rain,
And my danged old slicker's in the wagon train.
Come a ti, etc.*

*I jumped in the saddle and grabbed the horn,
I'm the best durned cowboy that ever was born.
Come a ti, etc.*

1. What famous cattle trail is mentioned in the song? _____

2. Where did this trail begin? Where did it end? _____

_____

3. The song refers to troubles on the trail. What were some of these troubles?

_____

4. Why did ranchers have cattle drives? _____

_____

5. Where were the cattle shipped at the end of the cattle trails? Why were they shipped

there? _____

_____

6. How did the railroad eventually bring the era of cattle drives to an end?

_____

_____

Life on the Great Plains

The excerpt below is from a letter written by Howard Ruede, a young homesteader in Kansas. Use the letter to help you complete the activity. For help, refer to pages 486 to 491 in your textbook.

This was another hot day, and we had heavy work too, laying up sod. Snyder broke a lot [area of sod] for us this A.M., and we began laying up the wall. . . . These "Kansas bricks" are from 2 to 4 inches thick, 12 [inches] wide, and 20 [inches] long, and the joints between them we fill with ground [dirt].

   We expect to get the roof in and have the place in condition to live in by the end of the week. The sod is heavy, and when you take 3 or 4 bricks on a litter [brick carrier] or hand barrow and carry it 50 to 150 feet, I tell you it is no easy work.

—Howard Ruede

Howard Ruede, *Sod-House Days: Letters from a Kansas Homesteader, 1877–78* (New York: Columbia University Press, 1937).

1. What is Howard Ruede describing in his letter?

_____

2. Why do you think he refers to the sod as "Kansas bricks"?

_____

_____

_____

3. What were people like Howard Ruede and his family called?

_____

4. What were some of the hardships these people faced?

_____

_____

_____

5. In spite of these hardships, why did people move to this part of the country?

_____

_____

_____

6. How did the Homestead Act of 1862 encourage people to settle in Kansas?

_____

_____

_____

7. What three advances in technology helped the people who were living on the Great Plains?

_____

_____

_____

Frame of Reference

A frame of reference is the basis of a person's point of view. Read the paragraphs below about two people. Then answer the questions about each person's point of view. For help, refer to pages 492 and 493 in your textbook.

José and his family are migrant workers. They do not have a permanent home. They move from place to place working on various farms picking crops.

Myra's family lives in a small town. The family has traveled outside their town rarely.

Here's how José and Myra feel about traveling.

José: I am tired of traveling. More than anything I would like to have a home. I would never leave it.

Myra: I am tired of living in my town. I want to see the world. More than anything, I would like to travel.

1. What is the frame of reference, or background, of José and Myra?

   _____

   _____

2. What are the points of view of José and Myra?

   _____

   _____

   _____

3. How does knowing each person's frame of reference help you understand his or her point of view on traveling?

   _____

   _____

   _____

©Macmillan/McGraw-Hill

Changes on the Plains

The statements on the right were made by Native American leaders. Use them to complete the activity. For help, refer to pages 494 to 499 in your textbook.

1. a. What change on the Plains is Crazy Horse describing?

_____

b. What caused the Native Americans to lose their land and buffalo?

_____

_____

2. a. What do you think Ten Bears is explaining with these words?

_____

_____

b. Why did the United States government begin forcing Native Americans onto reservations?

_____

_____

_____

3. a. When did Chief Joseph speak these words?

_____

_____

b. Why had he and other Native Americans been fighting American soldiers?

_____

_____

c. What was the result of the Plains Wars?

_____

_____

The Great Spirit gave us plenty of land to live on, and buffalo . . . and other game. But . . . you are killing off our game, so it is hard for us to live.

Crazy Horse

I was born upon the prairie where the wind blew free and there was nothing to break the light of the sun. . . . I want to die there and not within walls.

Ten Bears

Hear me, my chiefs. I am tired; my heart is sick and sad. From where the sun now stands I will fight no more forever.

Chief Joseph

Using New Words

Write each term from the box on the line next to its meaning. For help, refer to the lessons in Chapter 16 of your textbook.

cattle drive	railhead	reservation	transcontinental railroad
property rights	Custer's Last Stand	cowtowns	Pacific Railroad Act
homesteader	stockyard	Homestead Act	

1. offered two companies government loans and free land to build a transcontinental railroad across the United States _____

2. a long journey cowboys took to herd cattle from ranches in the West to the railroads _____

3. a town that sprang up along a new railroad line _____

4. a person who claimed land under the Homestead Act _____

5. a cattle pen _____

6. a railroad that crosses the entire continent _____

7. rights to own or use something—such as land. People could buy or sell land. _____

8. a territory reserved, or set aside, for Native Americans _____

9. gave 160 acres of public land to any adult man or widow if he or she farmed the land for five years _____

10. towns that developed for cowboys passing through _____

11. a battle where the Lakota, Cheyenne, and Arapaho fought against the U.S. Cavalry at Little Big Horn _____

Big Business

Draw a line from each picture to the description that matches it. Then answer the questions. For help, refer to pages 504 to 509 in your textbook.

1. a. This person invented the light bulb.

   b. Name another thing he invented.

   _____

2. a. This person invented the telephone.

   b. What led him to develop the telephone.

   _____

   _____

   _____

   _____

3. a. This person made a fortune in the oil business.

   b. Why was his oil company, Standard Oil, called a monopoly?

   _____

   _____

4. a. This person protested the use of child labor.

   b. What effect did her protest have?

   _____

   _____

   _____

5. a. This person founded a union.

   b. What weapon did he think important in fighting for workers' rights?

   _____

Mary Harris Jones

Alexander Graham Bell

John D. Rockefeller

Samuel Gompers

Thomas Alva Edison

Name: _____   Date: _____

Taking a Look at Immigration

Use the graph to answer the questions. For help, refer to pages 510 to 515 in your textbook.

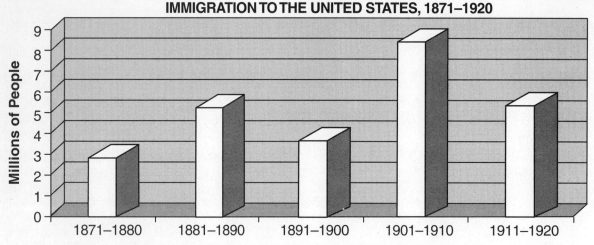

IMMIGRATION TO THE UNITED STATES, 1871–1920

1. About how many people immigrated to the United States during the period shown on the graph? _____

2. Between which years was the number of immigrants the largest? _____ About how many people immigrated during this period? _____

3. In which ways were the new immigrants different from those who had come before the Civil War? _____

   _____

   _____

   _____

4. Why did most of these immigrants come to the United States?

   _____

5. Where did most of the new immigrants settle and why did they settle there?

   _____

   _____

6. What was life like for immigrants living in cities? _____

   _____

   _____

©Macmillan/McGraw-Hill

Using Primary and Secondary Sources

Use the paragraphs on the right to complete the activity. For help, refer
to pages 516 and 517 in your textbook.

1. a. This paragraph is taken from the
autobiography of William Allen
White. White was the editor of the
Emporia Gazette, a newspaper
published in Emporia, Kansas.
Here he describes how his town
reacted to the Spanish-American
War. Is it a primary source or a
secondary source?

_____

b. How do you know?

_____

_____

_____

> The country was excited. Emporia
> was thrilled to the core. We
> celebrated the fall of Santiago with a
> big public meeting outdoors . . . and
> Ike Lambert . . . spoke to the
> multitude. . . . The band played "The
> Star-Spangled Banner," we sang
> "Hail Columbia," threw out a full-
> throated hymn to imperialism with the
> verses of "America," and were most
> pleased with ourselves.
>
> —William Allen White

2. a. This paragraph is from a book
written by an historian in 1982. It
describes how the American
people reacted to the Spanish-
American War. Is it a primary
source or a secondary source?

_____

b. How do you know?

_____

_____

_____

> On February 15 . . . a tremendous
> explosion rocked the [*Maine*]. . . .
>   Many Americans [believed] the
> Spanish had sunk the ship. . . .
>   The Spanish government claimed
> the disaster was caused by an
> explosion inside the *Maine*. . . .
>   In any case, a demand for war
> against Spain swept the United
> States. In New York City a man . . .
> proclaimed, "Remember the *Maine!*"
> This became a battle cry.
>
> —John A. Garraty

3. How do both these sources help you understand history? _____

_____

_____

_____

American Expansion in the 1800s

Use the map below to complete the activity. For help, refer to pages 518 to 521 in your textbook.

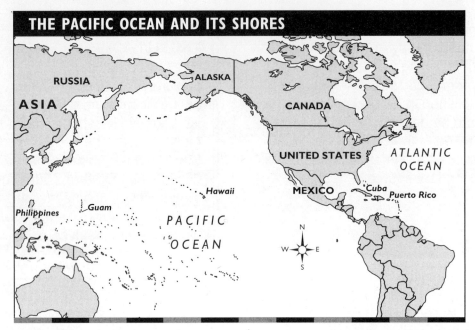

THE PACIFIC OCEAN AND ITS SHORES

1. **a.** Locate the territory the United States bought from Russia. Color it blue.

   b. List three valuable resources that are found there today.

   _____

2. **a.** Locate the islands where the English captain James Cook landed in 1778. Circle them.

   b. How did the United States gain these islands?

   _____

   _____

   _____

   _____

   _____

3. **a.** Locate the three territories that the United States gained as a result of the Spanish-American War. Circle them in red.

   b. What started this war?

   _____

   _____

   _____

   _____

   c. What eventually happened to the territories the United States gained?

   _____

   _____

   _____

   _____

The Times of Theodore Roosevelt

Each headline highlights an event that happened during the Presidency of Theodore Roosevelt. Read each headline. Then tell why each event was important. For help, refer to pages 522 to 527 in your textbook.

Roosevelt the Trust Buster

_____

_____

U.S. Builds Panama Canal

_____

_____

_____

Roosevelt Reforms the Food and Drug Industry

_____

_____

_____

Model T's Roll Off Assembly Line

_____

_____

_____

Roosevelt Sets Up National Parks

_____

_____

_____

Wright Brothers Take Off

_____

_____

Matching Words and Meanings

Write each term from the box on the line next to its meaning. For help, refer to the lessons in Chapter 17 of your textbook.

slum	monopoly	corporation	labor union	Spanish-American War
strike	tenement	sweatshop	national park	Great Chicago Fire
reform	Buffalo Soldiers	Rough Riders	assembly line	settlement house

_____ 1. a company that controls an entire industry

_____ 2. a large business that is owned by shareholders

_____ 3. a group of soldiers organized by Theodore Roosevelt to fight the Spanish in Cuba

_____ 4. a small factory often with unhealthy working conditions

_____ 5. an organization formed by workers to strive for better wages and working conditions

_____ 6. a period when all the workers in a business refuse to work until the owners meet their demands

_____ 7. a poor, crowded section of a city with rundown and unsafe housing

_____ 8. a building carved up into small apartments

_____ 9. a fire in 1871 that killed hundreds of people, left thousands homeless, and destroyed a third of Chicago

_____ 10. a community center that provides child care, education, and other services to the poor

_____ 11. a war fought in 1898 between the United States and Spain

_____ 12. changes designed to make things better

_____ 13. a way to manufacture a product quickly and cheaply by moving partially built products from one work area to another on a moving belt

_____ 14. African American cavalries

_____ 15. an area set aside for its natural beauty, where no one is allowed to live

Events of World War I

The newspaper headlines below might have appeared during World War I.
Read the headlines. Then write a sentence that explains each one.
For help, refer to pages 540 to 545 in your textbook.

Sinking of *Lusitania* Angers Americans

_____

_____

U.S. Declares War

_____

_____

A New Kind of War Is Fought in Europe

_____

_____

_____

Americans at Home Contribute to War Effort

_____

_____

_____

Allies Sign Treaty of Versailles

_____

_____

African Americans Move North

_____

_____

Looking at the Roaring Twenties

The pictures on the right show some of the changes that came about during the Roaring Twenties. Draw a line from each picture to the caption that describes it. Then answer the questions. For help, refer to pages 546 to 551 in your textbook.

The automobile brought people closer together and changed life in the U.S. and around the world. During the 1920s, many people bought automobiles for the first time. The first shopping center with a parking lot opened in 1924.

Media grew rapidly. On the radio people listened to the news, soap operas, and the rhythms of jazz. At the movies they cheered and laughed. The new technology created many heroes. Newspapers and magazines made people famous.

Suffrage leaders such as Carrie Chapman Catt used the media to spread their arguments for giving women the right to vote. Eventually the United States Congress passed the Nineteenth Amendment giving women this right.

1. Why was the ten-year period after World War I nicknamed the Roaring Twenties?

_____

2. Which groups of people did not benefit from the prosperity of the Roaring Twenties?

_____

_____

©Macmillan/McGraw-Hill

The Great Depression

Use the political cartoon on the right to complete the activity. For help, refer to pages 552 to 557 in your textbook.

1. What is the political cartoon about?

_____

_____

_____

_____

2. What term in the cartoon refers to the way that President Roosevelt wanted to cure the nation?

_____

3. What do the bottles on the table stand for?

_____

_____

_____

_____

4. Complete the chart below. Write what the initials of each New Deal program stand for and how the program helped put people to work.

PROGRAM	WHAT THE INITIALS STAND FOR	WHAT THE PROGRAM DID
WPA		
CCC		
TVA		

Events of World War II

Use the information in the box to complete the chart. Then answer the questions. For help, refer to pages 558 to 565 in your textbook.

> - Japan attacks Pearl Harbor. The United States declares war against Japan.
>
> - Allied troops invade Normandy on D-Day.
>
> - The United States drops atomic bombs on Hiroshima and Nagasaki. Japan surrenders. World War II ends.
>
> - Hitler attacks Poland. World War II begins.
>
> - Germany surrenders after Berlin falls.

| IMPORTANT EVENTS OF WORLD WAR II ||
DATE	EVENT
September 1939	
December 1941	
June 1944	
May 1945	
August 1945	

1. World War II was fought between the Axis and the Allied powers. Which countries formed each group.

Allied Powers: _____

Axis Powers: _____

2. Why did the Germans set up concentration camps?

_____

_____

©Macmillan/McGraw-Hill

The Postwar Years

Use the pictures on the right to complete the activity. For help, refer to pages 566 to 571 in your textbook.

1. a. Draw a line to the picture that represents the alliance formed among countries of Western Europe and the United States after World War II.

b. Why was this alliance created?

_____

_____

North Korea

South Korea

Korean War

2. a. Draw a line to the picture that represents a conflict that involved the United States in the 1950s.

b. What was the cause of this conflict?

_____

_____

_____

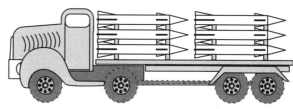

Arms Race

3. a. Draw a line to the picture that represents a competition between the United States and the Soviet Union.

b. What was its purpose?

_____

_____

_____

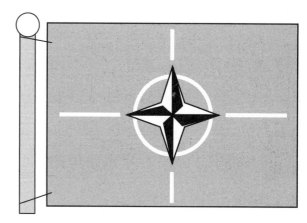

NATO

Drawing Conclusions

Follow the directions to complete the activity. For help, refer to pages 572 and 573 of your textbook.

Write the four steps in drawing conclusions.

1. _____

2. _____

3. _____

4. _____

Read the following paragraph. Then answer the questions. Circle your answer.

In the early 1950s, the United States and the Soviet Union began an arms race. Each nation worked to build the world's most powerful weapons to defend itself against the other. Many people feared a war involving atomic weapons. Some families even built bomb shelters in their backyards.

1. What is the subject of the information in the paragraph?

   families   bomb shelters   arms race

2. What connects the pieces of information?

   peace and love   fear and mistrust   backgrounds and bomb shelters

3. What conclusion can you draw?

   _____ The Soviet Union and the United States were preparing for war.

   _____ The Soviet Union wanted to build its economy.

   _____ The United States wanted to protect its families.

Matching Words and Their Meanings

Write the letter of each term from the box on the line next to its definition. For help, refer to the lessons in Chapter 18 of your textbook.

---

a. Allied Powers   **f.** Cold War   **k.** concentration camp   **p.** Central Powers

b. communism   **g.** Holocaust   **l.** League of Nations   **q.** Roaring Twenties

c. World War II   **h.** New Deal   **m.** League of Women Voters   **r.** Great Depression

d. Iron Curtain   **i.** arms race   **n.** Nineteenth Amendment   **s.** United Nations

e. Axis Powers   **j.** Treaty of Versailles   **o.** internment camp   **t.** discrimination

---

_____ 1. the World War I alliance that included Britain, France, Italy, Belgium, and Russia

_____ 2. the United States declared war on this alliance in World War I

_____ 3. ended World War I

_____ 4. the first organization in which countries united to prevent future wars

_____ 5. a decade of prosperity

_____ 6. a Constitutional amendment that gave women the vote

_____ 7. helps inform women and men about political issues

_____ 8. formed at the end of World War II to keep world peace

_____ 9. helped the United States recover from the Depression

_____ 10. the alliance formed when Japan, Italy, and Germany signed a treaty of friendship

_____ 11. the war fought between Great Britain and France against the Axis Powers

_____ 12. a social and political system in which all property is owned by the government

_____ 13. a place where people are imprisoned during wartime

_____ 14. a place where the Germans enslaved and murdered those they considered their enemies

_____ 15. Hitler's attempt to destroy the Jewish people

_____ 16. a war between the U.S. and the Soviet Union fought with ideas, words, money, and sometimes violence

_____ 17. the imaginary line dividing Europe into communist and noncommunist countries

_____ 18. a period of failed businesses and job loss

_____ 19. a race between the U.S. and the Soviet Union to build the most powerful weapons in the world

_____ 20. an unfair difference in treatment of people

©Macmillan/McGraw-Hill

People in the Civil Rights Movement

Draw a line from each paragraph to the person the paragraph describes. For help, refer to pages 578 to 583 in your textbook.

1. This lawyer argued *Brown* versus *Board of Education of Topeka, Kansas* before the Supreme Court. The Court ruled that segregated public schools were illegal.

Lyndon Johnson

2. This woman was arrested for not giving up her seat in the white section of a Montgomery bus. To support her, African Americans in Montgomery boycotted the buses. A year later the Supreme Court ordered Montgomery to end segregation on its buses.

Martin Luther King, Jr.

3. This man called for a peaceful march on Washington, D.C. Its great success drew national attention to the civil rights movement, and the movement continued to grow across the nation.

Rosa Parks

4. This man worked hard to convince Congress to pass the Civil Rights Act of 1964 and the Voting Rights Act of 1965. These acts helped African Americans get elected to government offices.

Thurgood Marshall

©Macmillan/McGraw-Hill

Our Nation

Practice and Activity

A Decade of Change

Read the following statements. Label each statement **True** or **False**.
Then write the reason for your answer. For help, refer to pages 584 to 587
in your textbook.

1. The United States suffered a great
blow when President Kennedy was
killed on November 22, 1963.

_____

_____

_____

_____

_____

John F. Kennedy

2. Migrant farm workers were one group
that did not suffer from poverty and
discrimination.

_____

_____

_____

_____

_____

_____

3. During the 1960s, poverty and discrimination drew the attention of many leaders.

_____

_____

_____

_____

4. By the end of the 1960s, most Americans supported the Vietnam War.

_____

_____

©Macmillan/McGraw-Hill

Change Since 1972

Use the information in the box to complete the chart. For help, refer to pages 590 to 597 in your textbook. The first event has been filled in for you.

> • Leaders of Egypt and Israel sign a peace treaty in Washington, D.C.
>
> • The Soviet Union breaks up into 15 independent republics, thereby ending the Cold War.
>
> • Sandra Day O'Connor becomes the first woman named to the United States Supreme Court.
>
> • Leaders of the United States and the Soviet Union sign an arms treaty agreeing to destroy some of their nuclear missiles.
>
> • The Berlin Wall, a symbol of the Iron Curtain, is torn down.
>
> • Nixon becomes the first United States President to visit China.
>
> • The Americans With Disabilities Act becomes a law.

DATE	EVENT
1972	Nixon becomes the first United States President to visit China.
1979	
1981	
1987	
1989	
1990	
1991	

Using Reference Sources

Suppose you are writing a report about the Mexican War. Draw a line from the information you want to find to the picture that shows where to find it. Then give a reason for choosing that reference source. For help, refer to pages 598 and 599 in your textbook.

1. You want to find a map that shows key battles in the Mexican War.

Reason: _____

_____

2. You need to find general information about General Winfield Scott.

Reason: _____

_____

_____

How would you find the information?

_____

_____

3. You want to find a book about Zachary Taylor, but don't have a title.

Reason: _____

_____

How would you find the book you want?

_____

_____

_____

4. You want to find some geographical information about Mexico.

Reason: _____

_____

_____

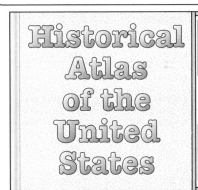

Card Catalog

Enter Subject:
Taylor, Zachary

Press: ↵ Return

Historical Atlas of the United States

Atlas of the World

Encyclopedia

Challenging the Future

Answer the questions to complete the activity. For help, refer to pages 600 to 603 in your textbook.

1. a. What threat to national security has become a problem in the United States?

_____

b. Explain the first threat to security on American soil.

_____

_____

_____

_____

c. Describe briefly the events of September 11, 2001. What made these events so devastating?

_____

_____

_____

_____

_____

d. What lies behind the attacks on our nation?

_____

_____

2. a. How many foreign-born Americans were counted during the census in 2000? _____

b. Traditionally, how have immigrants contributed to our country?

_____

_____

_____

3. What happened on July 20, 1969, to achieve a president's goal?

_____

_____

_____

4. What joint effort allows the United States to explore space today?

_____

_____

_____

_____

5. What is a major area of research in the field of medicine? (Circle one)

genetics   crime   research

6. What part does the computer play in today's world?

_____

_____

©Macmillan/McGraw-Hill

Name: _____   Date: _____

Thinking About New Terms

The vowels have been left out of the terms below. Write each term correctly.
Then write the number of the definition in the circle next to the term it defines.
For help, refer to the lessons in Chapter 19 of your textbook.

a. Cvl Rghts ct f 1964   ◯
_____

_____

b. L Cs   ◯
_____

c. ntgrt   ◯
_____

d. Vtnm Wr   ◯
_____

e. Wtrgt Scndl   ◯
_____

f. mrcns Wth Dsblts ct   ◯
_____

_____

g. Prsn Glf Wr   ◯
_____

h. ctvst   ◯
_____

i. trrrsm   ◯
_____

j. Vtng Rghts ct   ◯
_____

1. a law that makes it illegal for employers to discriminate against people with disabilities

2. a scandal that involved President Nixon and his campaign workers spying on his opponents

3. a war against Iraq for invading the country of Kuwait

4. the war between the United States and the communist country of North Vietnam over North Vietnam's expansion into South Vietnam

5. a person who uses action for political goals

6. to bring blacks and whites together

7. the use of fear and violence to gain political goals

8. the farm workers' struggle for a better life

9. the law that protects the right of African Americans to vote

10. the law that makes segregation illegal in public places, including hotels, theaters, playgrounds, and libraries

©Macmillan/McGraw-Hill

Traveling Through Canada

Use the map below to complete the activity. For help, refer to pages 610 to 615 in your textbook.

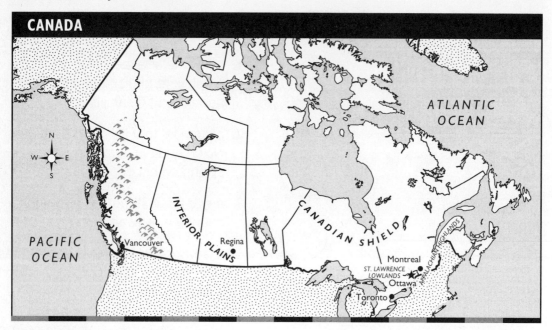

CANADA

ATLANTIC OCEAN

INTERIOR PLAINS

CANADIAN SHIELD

PACIFIC OCEAN

Vancouver

Regina

APPALACHIAN HIGHLANDS

Montreal

ST. LAWRENCE LOWLANDS

Ottawa

Toronto

1. **a.** Suppose you and your family are traveling across Canada. You begin your trip in Nova Scotia. Label Nova Scotia on the map.

   b. Which hilly wooded region lies west of Nova Scotia?

   _____

   _____

2. **a.** From Nova Scotia you travel to Montreal and then to Toronto. Underline Montreal and Toronto on the map.

   b. In which region are these cities located?

   _____

   _____

3. **a.** From Toronto you travel to Regina. Put a box around this city on the map.

   b. In which region is this city located?

   _____

   c. Which region did you cross on your way from Toronto to Regina?

   _____

4. **a.** You end your trip in Vancouver. Put a star next to this city on the map.

   b. Label the mountainous region you crossed on your way to Vancouver.

5. **a.** Label Canada's most recent territory.

   b. Which native people make up 85 percent of the population in this territory?

   _____

©Macmillan/McGraw-Hill

A View of Mexico

Use the map to complete the activity. For help, refer to pages 616
to 621 in your textbook.

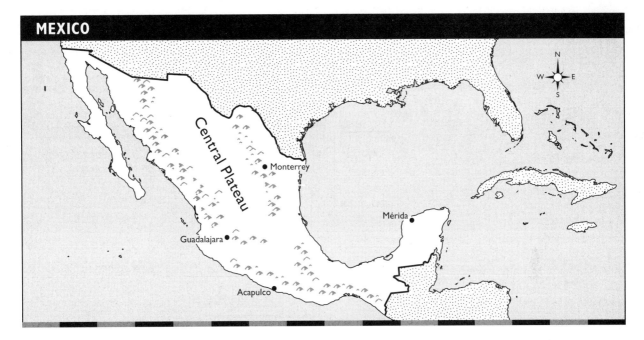

MEXICO

Central Plateau

• Monterrey

• Mérida

Guadalajara •

Acapulco •

1. Label the following bodies of water on
   the map.

   Gulf of Mexico   Pacific Ocean

2. Label the following geographic regions.

   Western Sierra Madre
   Eastern Sierra Madre
   Yucatán Peninsula
   Sonora Desert

3. How would you describe the climate in
   the Yucatán Peninsula?

   _____

   _____

   _____

4. What kind of forest covers part of the
   Yucatán Peninsula?

   _____

5. Locate and label the capital city of
   Mexico.

6. Locate the region where most of
   Mexico's people live. Circle it.

7. From which two groups of people are
   most Mexicans descended?

   _____

   _____

8. How has the history of Mexico affected
   its culture?

   _____

   _____

   _____

Name: _____ Date: _____

Central America and the Caribbean

Use the map to complete the activity. For help, refer to pages 622 to 627 in your textbook.

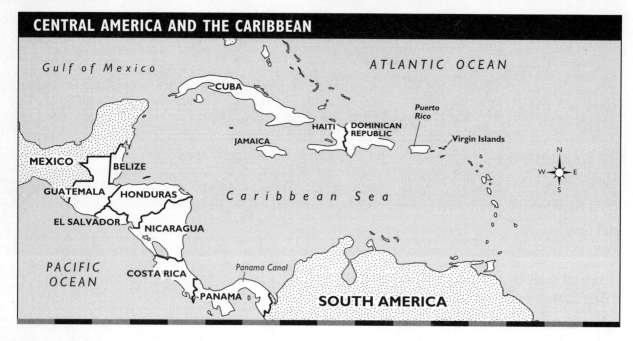

CENTRAL AMERICA AND THE CARIBBEAN

Gulf of Mexico · ATLANTIC OCEAN · CUBA · Puerto Rico · HAITI · DOMINICAN REPUBLIC · Virgin Islands · JAMAICA · MEXICO · BELIZE · GUATEMALA · HONDURAS · Caribbean Sea · EL SALVADOR · NICARAGUA · PACIFIC OCEAN · COSTA RICA · Panama Canal · PANAMA · SOUTH AMERICA

1. Locate the Caribbean islands and color them yellow. Locate Central America and color it red.

2. Write the letter of each statement next to the spot on the map it describes.

   A. Large parts of these three Central American countries are covered with rain forests.

   B. This is an important trade route for the United States.

   C. This island is a United States commonwealth.

   D. Large numbers of people in this Central American country have African roots.

   E. The people of this Caribbean country speak a mixture of French and African languages.

3. What kind of climate do most of the countries in this area have?

   _____

4. How would you describe the geography of this area? _____

   _____

   _____

5. Who are the ancestors of most of the people who live in this area?

   _____

Name: _____   Date: _____

South America

Use the map on the right to complete the activity. For help, refer to pages 628 to 633 in your textbook.

1. Draw and label the equator on the map. Which three South American countries does the equator pass through?

   _____

   _____

2. How are the seasons south of the equator different from the seasons in the United States?

   _____

   _____

3. Locate and label the longest unbroken mountain chain in the world.

   What empire once stretched along 2,500 miles of these mountains?

   _____

4. Locate and label the pampas.

5. Locate and label the region of the world's largest tropical rain forest. Why is this rain forest important?

   _____

   _____

6. Locate and label the second longest river in the world. What is the course of this river?

   _____

   _____

7. What four cultures have made major contributions to the population of South America?

   _____

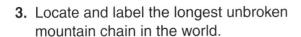
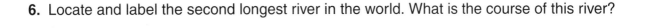

SOUTH AMERICA

VENEZUELA
GUYANA
SURINAME
FRENCH GUIANA
COLOMBIA
ECUADOR
PERU
BRAZIL
BOLIVIA
PACIFIC OCEAN
CHILE
PARAGUAY
ARGENTINA
URUGUAY
ATLANTIC OCEAN

N
W   E
S

©Macmillan/McGraw-Hill

Matching Words and Meanings

Write the letter of each term next to its meaning. For help, refer to the lessons in Unit 9 of your textbook.

a. bilingual	**d.** mestizo	**g.** commonwealth
b. hurricane	**e.** rain forest	**h.** favela
c. province	**f.** North American Free Trade Agreement	**i.** inflation

_____ **1.** speaking or writing in two languages

_____ **2.** a territory in Canada that has its own government, like the states in the United States

_____ **3.** an agreement signed by Canada, the United States and Mexico to boost trade among the three neighbors and to bring about greater economic interdependence

_____ **4.** a forest that receives lots of rain year-round

_____ **5.** a person of mixed European and Indian ancestry

_____ **6.** a violent storm with powerful winds and enormous waves

_____ **7.** a rise in the prices of goods and services

_____ **8.** a country or state governed by its own people but voluntarily united with the United States

_____ **9.** a slum area of Brazil

Activities

Art

- Working in a group, choose a culture that you learned about in this unit, such as the Maya or Hopi. Then on a sheet of oaktag, create a mural about that culture.

- Review what you learned about the culture. What kind of structures did they live in? Were they farmers? What crops did they grow? What else was interesting or unique about them?

- Make sketches on the oaktag showing these important details. Then use paint, glitter, beans, pasta, corn, and seeds to make your mural come alive.

- Be sure to label your mural and write a description below each picture. Share your mural with the class.

Map Early Native Americans

- Working in groups, trace a large map of the United States. Cut it out and paste it onto a large piece of oaktag. Using markers—a different color for each region—outline the four regions of the country in which early Native Americans lived: West, Southwest, Plains, and Woodlands. Label each region.

- Now use the markers to draw the geographical features of each region on the map.

- On construction paper, draw scenes showing life among cultures of each region. You might want to show the kinds of structures the Native Americans lived in, the types of clothes they wore, or how they farmed. Cut out the pictures. Paste the cutouts onto the map in the proper place.

- Make sure you label your map and write a caption below each scene you've drawn. Share your map with the class.

Language Arts

- Work in groups to create a news broadcast telling the story of the first Thanksgiving in Plymouth Colony. One person in each group can take the role of the news announcer. The others can act out the events in the story.

- Work with your group to write what the announcer will say. Then plan and write the scenes. The announcer should describe the reasons the feast was held, the meal the Pilgrims and Native Americans ate, and other activities that took place.

- The scenes should demonstrate some of the Pilgrim and Native American activities, such as preparing the food. You might want to bring in props to use for the meal.

- Practice your news broadcast and then share it with the class.

Map Exploration

- Trace a map of the world and cut it out. Then paste it onto a large piece of oaktag.

- Choose any explorer you read about in this unit and draw a picture of him on construction paper. Cut it out. Paste the picture near the country from which the explorer set out. Draw a line connecting the picture and the country.

- Now draw the explorer's route to North America on the map. Draw a series of stars. Cut them out, paste a star near each place the explorer landed.

- Draw small pictures of what the explorer saw during his expeditions. Paste the pictures onto your map near the places where the things were seen.

- Make sure you label your map and write descriptions of what the explorer saw. Present your map to the class.

Language Arts

- Working in pairs, interview a person you have learned about in this unit. Choose a person in whom both of you are interested, such as Anne Hutchinson or Benjamin Franklin.

- Review what you have learned about the person. Write a series of questions to ask him or her. Also write the person's answers to the questions. Think about the times in which the person lived as you write the answers.

- Have one partner act as the interviewer and the other act as the person being interviewed. Practice your interview, then conduct the interview in front of the class.

Map the 13 Colonies

- Trace a map of the original 13 colonies of the United States. Then cut it out and paste the map onto a large piece of oaktag.

- Label each colony on your map. Then draw or cut out pictures that help identify each colony. You may draw anything that describes the colony, such as goods that the colony produced or one of the leaders of the colony.

- Paste the pictures near the appropriate colony on your map. Present your map to the class.

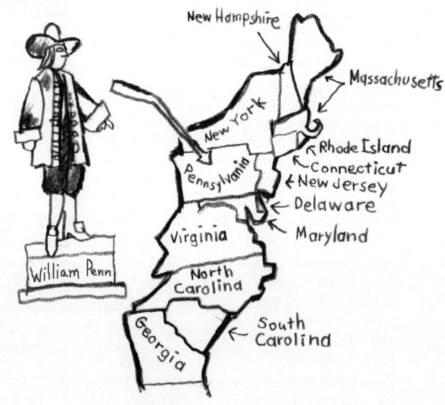

Language Arts

- Working in groups of four, write a play about the Constitutional Convention.

- Review what you learned about the Convention in this unit. Think about the important topics discussed at the Convention as you decide what to cover in your play. Choose the characters you want to be in your play. Write the words the characters will say. Assign each character to one person in your group. If there are more than four characters in your play, some members of your group can play more than one role.

- Decide on and collect various props.

- Rehearse your play and present it to the class.

Diagram a Historical Battle

- Use maps and diagrams to record the events of a Revolutionary War battle.

- Choose one battle that you read about in this unit. Map out, on a large sheet of paper, the section of the United States in which the battle took place. Cut out the map and paste it onto a piece of oaktag. Label the states you've included, as well as the state capitals and the cities near to the battle site.

- Label and illustrate the battle site. Use markers of different colors to draw soldiers fighting on different sides. You may also wish to draw the artillery used.

- Write a title for your diagram, including the date on which the battle took place. On a separate sheet of paper, write an explanation of the major events and the final outcome of the battle. Glue it onto the diagram.

- Show your battle diagram to the class.

Language Arts

- Work in pairs to interview a person who might have lived during the period of time you read about in this unit. You might choose

    ○ a pioneer heading west of the Appalachians in 1775

    ○ a southerner moving to Texas in the 1850s

    ○ a forty niner looking for gold in California.

- Working with your partner, write interview questions for the interviewee. Be sure to include questions about the person's personal life, the purpose of the journey, and what the person expected to find. Then write answers to the questions you've written.

- Take turns role-playing the interviewer and interviewee. After practicing your interview, perform it for the class.

Map the United States of 1803

- Draw a political map to show the United States today and in the early 1800s.

- Trace a map of the United States on a large piece of paper. Include outlines and labels of the 48 mainland states. Paste the map on a large piece of oaktag.

- Using the information you learned in this chapter, alter the map to show the country as it looked in 1803. Think about the ways in which the country was divided at that time. Use colored pencils to color in the different regions of the country. Then label each region.

- Make a map key to identify the different regions shown on your map. Display your map for the class to see.

©Macmillan/McGraw-Hill

Language Arts

- Work in groups of three to write the diary of a slave who lived during the period of time you learned about in this unit.

- As you review the information in the unit, think about the events you studied from the point of view of a slave. What kinds of thoughts and feelings do you think a slave would have had before the Civil War started, while the war was going on, and during Reconstruction?

- Divide the diary into three parts—before the Civil War, during the Civil War, and Reconstruction. Assign one part to each member of your group.

- When you finish writing, read each part of the diary and make sure it makes sense. Then share it with your class.

Create a Civil War Monument

- Work in small groups to create a Civil War monument in the form of a drum.

- Review the battles of the Civil War you read about in this unit. Choose one battle and write some facts about it. Include information about where the battle took place, its outcome, and what affect the battle had on the war.

- Paste the facts onto a large sheet of oaktag. Add pictures to the oaktag. Show key leaders of the battle. Label each picture. Decorate the oaktag with red, white and blue stars. Paste a one-inch-wide strip of black construction paper across the top and bottom of the oaktag.

- Roll the piece of oaktag so that one edge overlaps the other slightly. Then tape the oaktag together. Next punch holes along the rim on the top and bottom of the rolled up oaktag. Weave string through the holes, from top to bottom, around the drum. Stand up your monument. Explain it to the class.

The Battle of Gettysburg

Science

- Research one of the many items invented during the late 1800s. Find out how it was invented, who invented it, what it was used for, and how this invention affected the people who used it.

- Pretend that you are introducing this invention to the public for the first time at a world's fair. Make a diagram of the invention. Label its features and write a description of how it works.

- Share the information about and diagram of the invention with your classmates. Explain how the invention will change their lives.

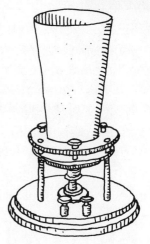

The First Telephone

Draw a Population Bar Graph

- Choose three cities or states in which the population grew as a result of the transcontinental railroad, immigration, or other factors.

- Research the population of each place during 1850 and 1880. Using markers of different colors, make a bar graph that shows the increase in population for each place.

- Indicate on your graph the possible reasons for the increase in population. Give your graph a title. Share your graph with the class.

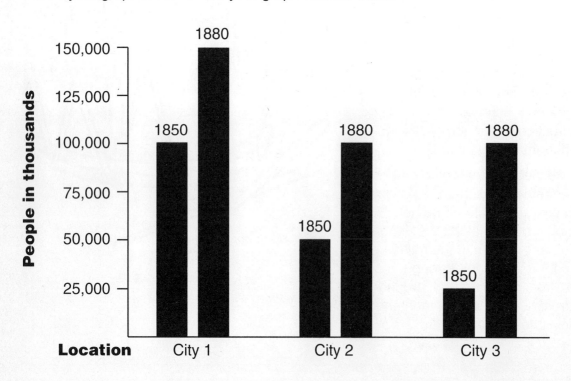

©Macmillan/McGraw-Hill

Language Arts

- Review what you learned in the unit about how women won the right to vote. You may use library reference sources for additional information.

- Working in a group, list the reasons people should vote. Include reasons discussed in the unit as well as your own.

- Use your list of reasons to create an "Everyone Should Vote" campaign to present to your classmates. Think about ways to get your message across. You might want to create a poster that lists reasons to vote. You also could create pamphlets or a banner, make stickers or buttons.

- Present your "Everyone Should Vote" campaign to the class.

Map Events of World War II

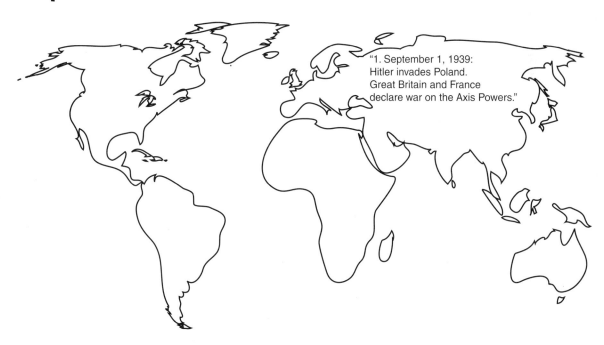

"1. September 1, 1939: Hitler invades Poland. Great Britain and France declare war on the Axis Powers."

- Working in groups, show the sequence of events that took place during World War II.

- Trace a large map of the world. Cut it out and paste it onto a piece of oaktag.

- Review what you learned about World War II in this unit. Using different color pencils, mark each event on the map. Number the events in the order they occurred. Give the date and a brief description of the event. You might want to color-code the events by marking battles won by the Axis countries in one color and those won by Allied countries in another color.

- Present your map to the class.

Art

- Create a travel brochure for one of the countries or regions you learned about in this unit.

- First choose a region on which you would like to focus. Then research the area and list some of its more interesting features, including geographic and historical sites, such as volcanoes and ancient ruins.

- Then fold a sheet of colored paper into three sections. On the outside fold, write the name of the place you are describing. Beneath the name draw a picture of the place.

- On the inside folds, write facts about the subject of your brochure. Describe the sites visitors would enjoy seeing. Include pictures to make the brochure attractive.

- When you're finished, show your brochure to your class.

Chart the Western Hemisphere

- Create a chart of the Western Hemisphere. Divide a sheet of large oaktag into three columns. Label the columns as follows.

Regions	Geography/Climate	People

- Fill in each column with as much information as you can from this unit. Make sure you include the United States as one of your regions.

- Illustrate your chart with drawings or pictures that relate to the information in each column. For instance, you might want to draw a picture of a volcano when describing the geography of Central America and the Caribbean. You could include an outline map of Brazil on which you've traced the course of the Amazon River—or an outline map of the United States on which you've traced the course of the Mississippi River.

Our Nation's Symbols: American Flag

Our Nation's Symbols: White House

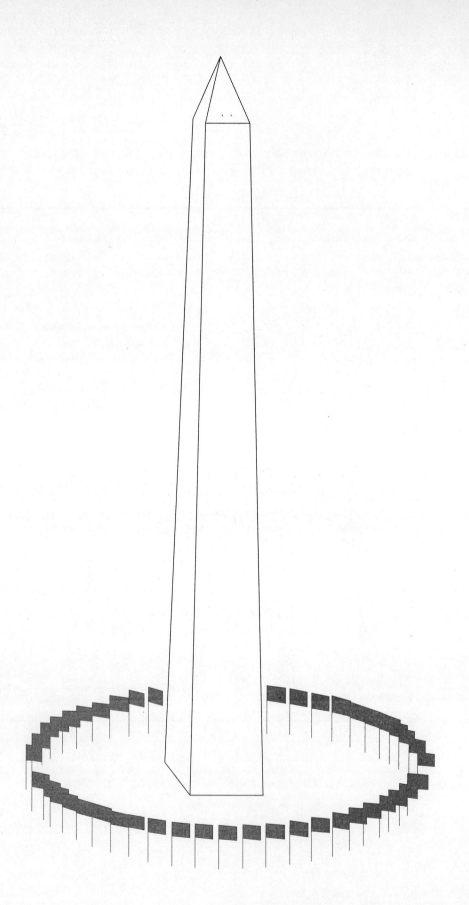

Our Nation's Symbols: Washington Monument

Our Nation's Symbols: Lincoln Memorial

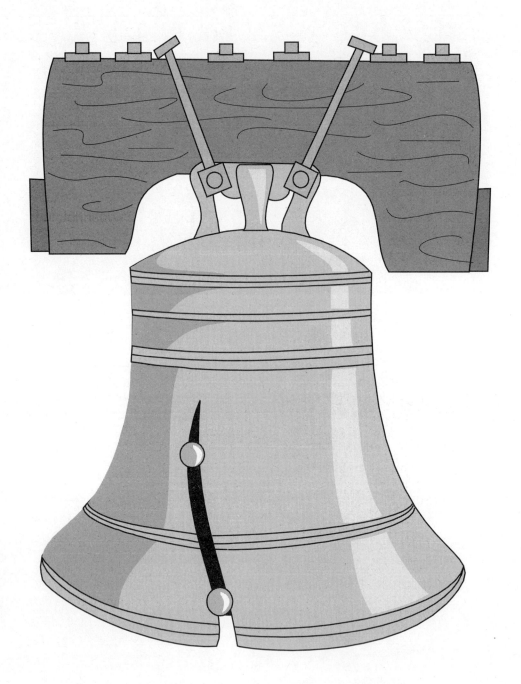